BENEATH THE

Caitlin Press Inc.
3375 Ponderosa Way
Qualicum Beach, BC V9K 2J8
www.caitlin-press.com

Text and cover design by Vici Johnstone
Cover images: Fernie-Fort Steele Brewing Company promotional calendar, c. 1909/1910.
Ruins of the Fort Steel Brewery, August 1, 1908. Fernie & District Historical Society, 1358.
Edited by Pam Roberts

Printed in Canada

Caitlin Press Inc. acknowledges financial support from the Government of Canada
and the Canada Council for the Arts, and the Province of British Columbia through
the British Columbia Arts Council and the Book Publisher's Tax Credit.

Library and Archives Canada Cataloguing in Publication

Beneath the coal dust : historical journeys through the Elk Valley and Crowsnest
Pass /
    Wayne Norton.
Norton, Wayne R. (Wayne Reid), 1948- author.

Canadiana 20220227748 | ISBN 9781773860923 (softcover)
LCSH: Elk River Valley (B.C.)—History. | LCSH: Crowsnest Pass (Alta. and B.C.)—
History. | LCSH: Coal mines and mining—British Columbia—Elk River Valley—
History. | LCSH: Coal mines and mining—Crowsnest Pass (Alta. and B.C.)—Histo-
ry. | LCC FC3845.E44 N67 2022 | DDC 971.1/65—dc23

BENEATH THE COAL DUST

HISTORICAL JOURNEYS THROUGH
THE ELK VALLEY AND CROWSNEST PASS

WAYNE NORTON

CAITLIN PRESS 2022

CONTENTS

MAP OF THE ELK VALLEY AND CROWSNEST PASS

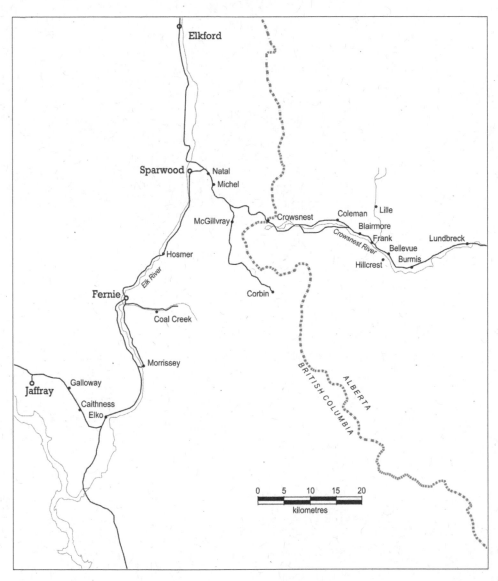

Map courtesy Mader and Associates

INTRODUCTION

All journeys begin somewhere. Those chronicled in this collection began for me with childhood visits to my grandfather in Fernie. Brief holidays created a lasting affection for the Elk Valley, which seemed a magical place of mountains and fishing adventures up Coal Creek, so different from the Royal Canadian Air Force bases where I was growing up in the 1950s and 1960s. My interest in history came much later and my fascination with local history later still. These articles are the result of that fascination.

In my book *Fernie at War*, I make the claim that the history of Fernie is the history of Canada during the Great War. I stand by that claim. If it happened in Canada in 1914 to 1919, it happened in Fernie. The experience of Fernie during those years should attract attention from people who otherwise would have no particular interest in a small East Kootenay community. I make no such grandiose assertion for this collection of articles. This is a book of local history, intended for those interested not necessarily in the broad sweep of national history, but rather in the smaller stories that are specific to an isolated and unique geographic region. And instead of dealing with the core regional narrative surrounding coal mining, these explorations attempt to see some of what has been neglected and hidden by that narrative—as the title *Beneath the Coal Dust* is intended to suggest.

As every traveller knows, a journey is fundamentally a personal experience. What proves to be central to the experience of one person may well be inconsequential to another; where one may find an easy hike, another might encounter insurmountable difficulty. The historical journeys offered here are no different. Some are intended to be casual strolls on a sunny Sunday afternoon. The traveller will return home still full of vim and vigour. Others demand more effort and may be disquieting. Most are pathways new to me, but occasionally I found myself on familiar ground where a word or two about previous journeys seemed appropriate. The advice given to anyone writing about history is that personal comments should be avoided. While that is sound advice, I hope readers will find the few occasions when I ignore it not too obtrusive.

Anyone following trails in the Elk Valley—historic or other- wise—should know those trails are within the unceded traditional territory of the Ktunaxa Nation. Yet everyone mentioned in the jour- neys undertaken for this book seems either to have been unaware of that fact or little troubled by it. Local historical writing affirms a narrative that begins with the foundational settler myth around the "discovery" of coal deposits, explains the absence of a Ktunaxa pres- ence on the resultant curse placed on the valley, and ends by celebrat- ing the ceremonial lifting of the curse in 1964. Apart from reports of participation in civic celebrations such as Dominion Day and Victoria Day, substantial mention of the Ktunaxa people is absent from con- temporary newspapers and from the literature on local history. Of all the regional historical paths that are yet to be explored—and there are many—the relationship of the Ktunaxa Nation to the Elk Valley stands paramount.

As any journey unfolds, many people offer roadside advice and assistance. I am grateful to all those who provided such to me, espe- cially on those occasions when I was losing my sense of direction. Foremost amongst these is Cory Dvorak. Without his generous con- tribution of time and expertise, this collection would not have been possible. I must also particularly thank Michael Saad for editorial suggestions, as well as Tom Langford, John Kinnear, Greg Nester- off, Alan Livingstone MacLeod, Ronald Greene, Philip Francis, Rein Stamm, Valerie Norton and Tanya Vaughan. Throughout the many twists and turns of transforming a writer's thoughts into print on the page, Vici Johnstone and her team at Caitlin Press have again earned my respect and gratitude. Editor Pam Robertson's remarkable atten- tion to detail has saved me from many an embarrassing error. Any that remain, of course, are entirely my responsibility.

Three articles require detailed acknowledgements. "Sedition at Michel" is a revision of "Identifying the Enemy: The Tale of Herman Elmer," which appeared in *British Columbia History* (volume 52, num- ber 4) and received the Anne and Philip Yandle Best Article Award from the British Columbia Historical Federation in 2019. For their as- sistance, I am very much indebted to Don McNair of Vernon, Tom Langford of Calgary, Dan Ste-Marie of Fernie and Andrea Lister, former editor of *British Columbia History*. "Empire of Suds" is a revision of "Judicious Control of the Malt Product: Albert Mutz in Coal Country," which appeared in *Brewery History*, number 185 (Winter 2020). I am grateful for the assistance of journal editor Tim Holt and for the essential information provided by beer historians Gary Flynn of Bellingham, the late Frank Mrazik of Montreal, Sean Enns of Nanaimo, Joe Wiebe and the late Greg Evans of Victoria, and Stan Sherstobitoff of Nelson. "Pretty Good Stuff" first appeared as "The Working Man's Beer" in *Canada's History* (June 2022) and is included here by permission. My thanks to senior editor Kate Jaimet for her many helpful suggestions.

My hope is that these articles might provide some signposts for others interested in embarking on historical journeys of their own. Whether those journeys are to be undertaken in the Elk Valley and Crowsnest Pass or elsewhere, I am tempted to offer travellers a word of advice. Be aware that signage can show where you are headed and perhaps indicate how far ahead your destination might be, but it can only hint at what you might find there.

Fernie & District Historical Society 4902do

"Healthy, Manly Sport"

The Crow's Nest Pass Football League

One of the ironies of the immigrant experience in Canada is that, having left home in hopes of a better life, attempts to create the old country experience in the new land were undertaken as soon as possible. The realm of competitive sport was no exception. To British Columbia and Alberta, Canadians from the East brought ice hockey and lacrosse; the Americans brought baseball, and the Italians bocce. The predominant British immigrant community imported rugby, polo, cricket and football. Each of these had its enthusiasts in East Kootenay and the Crowsnest Pass, but it was the working-class game of football that quickly rose to prominence.

As the largest communities in East Kootenay, Fernie and Cranbrook took the lead in establishing pastimes and competitions. Sports were played very early in the century on makeshift grounds, with community-based teams competing on Empire Day, Dominion Day and Labour Day. For Fernie's sports teams, their baseball, lacrosse and football opponents were then located to the west in Cranbrook or to the east in Pincher Creek and Lethbridge. The first football games involving an Elk Valley team occurred in May 1900 when Fernie took on Pincher Creek in the marquee event of the community's first Empire Day program, and then played a second match against Cranbrook. The games were given extensive coverage in the *Fernie Free Press*.[1] At the Labour Day celebrations of 1901 organized by the local miners' union—in addition to the region's first game of cricket being played and the chief focus of the day being on lacrosse—Fernie played host to Blairmore for a game of football. The significance was not immediately apparent, but that match was a small first step toward the emergence of a local sports tradition founded entirely on coal-based communities.

Members of the ragtag Fernie football team of 1901 pose for a commemorative photograph. Fernie & District Historical Society FFP (01)-0094

Over the next two years, occasional football games were played and the Fernie Amateur Athletic Association reserved two days a week for scrimmages on its sports field. The association eagerly accepted an invitation in 1903 to form a football league with communities all along the CPR rail line as far as Medicine Hat, but plans for the league did not proceed.[2] In the Alberta Crowsnest region, Coleman organized a team, looking to nearby Pass communities for opponents. In the British Columbia Crowsnest, Michel also formed a team and recorded its first victory at the Fourth of July sports program of 1903 in Fernie. However, baseball and lacrosse remained the more popular sports in Fernie, always on the programs of holiday events. For external competition, Fernie's baseball club typically began to look to Kalispell and the lacrosse club most often to Lethbridge.

Football enthusiasts could soon look closer to home. At a meeting in Coleman in May 1904, the Crow's Nest Pass Football League (CNPFL) was created. Some enthusiasts were forced to remain on the sidelines, however. Players at Morrissey, having just made an arrangement "for the immediate purchase of a ball," reluctantly admitted they were not ready to participate.[3] However, the new league declared its geographic limits were to be Morrissey to Macleod and announced the dates of an eight-game schedule for each of its five founding clubs: Fernie, Michel, Coleman, Blairmore and Pincher Creek. Playing under the system of rules developed in England known as Association Football, a team would receive two points for a win, one for a draw and none for a loss. The team with most points at the end of the season would be declared league champion. Each club contributed $15 toward medals that were to be awarded to members of the team with the most points when league competition concluded on August 3.[4]

The creation of the league was more an indication of enthusiasm than of preparedness. The first league matches were played on all-purpose sports fields of varying sizes and quality. Although rules were in place, standards were vague and play did not begin well. The *Fernie Free Press* described the first game between Fernie and Michel as "a fiasco." Because there were no nets or goalposts yet in place at Michel, flags were placed appropriately. A goal was awarded when, in the judgment of the referee, a player had been able "to send the sphere between the flags" at a proper height. At half-time, the Fernie team walked off the field in protest, insisting Michel had been given two goals that were actually wide of the mark. And so began what would prove to be recurrent administrative headaches for the CNP-FL.[5] However, both on and off the pitch, the first season was a success for the league in general and for the Fernie club in particular. With only one loss—recorded when their protest against Michel failed— the Fernie Football Club (Fernie FC) claimed the championship and league medals.

Patterns of administration and fundraising that would be followed year to year developed almost immediately. In early spring, the league executive invited delegates from clubs intending to enter league play to attend an organizational meeting, where new table officers were elected and a schedule of fixtures established. Individual clubs also held their organizational meetings in early spring. The key question for each club each year was whether or not personnel and finances were sufficient to participate in league play. Once a commitment was made, the discussion turned to the crucial details of fundraising. Club members paid a fee—perhaps 50 cents a month or a dollar for the season—and knew gate receipts from home games would provide substantial income. But they also knew that would not be enough. In addition to the costs of league membership, each club was responsible for its own travel expenses for away matches and for the accommodation expenses of visiting teams. Typically, club members would canvas local businesses and individuals for subscriptions or host a dinner and dance.

The most popular fundraiser was what was known as a basket social. Whether preceded by a dinner or followed by a dance, this became the most efficient means of raising money and was the only event in the football calendar that involved the women of the community. Responsible for the dinner and serving as the necessary dance partners, women were also called upon to create the baskets. On one occasion, Fernie FC appealed for assistance thus: "Any lady desirous of helping the club may do so by sending a basket to be auctioned and every young man should get his best girl busy on some unique production

---

Registered Clubs of the CNPFL, 1904 to 1915*

1904 Blairmore, Coleman, Fernie, Michel, Pincher Creek

1905 Coal Creek, Coleman, Fernie, Frank, Michel

1906 Coal Creek, Coleman, Fernie, Frank, Michel

1907 Coal Creek, Coleman, Fernie, Michel

1908 Bellevue, Coal Creek, Coleman, Fernie, Hosmer, Michel

1909 Bellevue, Coal Creek, Coleman, *Cowley, Fernie, Frank, Hosmer, Michel

1910 Bellevue, Coal Creek, Coleman, Fernie, Frank, Hosmer, Michel

1911 Bellevue, Coal Creek, Coleman, Frank, Michel

1912 Bellevue, Coal Creek, Coleman, Fernie, Hosmer, Michel

1913 Bellevue, *Blairmore, Coal Creek, Coleman, Fernie, Hillcrest, Hosmer, Michel

1914 *Bellevue, Coal Creek, Coleman, Corbin, Fernie, Frank, *Hillcrest, *Hosmer, Michel

1915 Coal Creek, Coleman, Fernie, Frank, Michel

* Starred names withdrew before the end of league play

of basket novelty." The appeal was successful: thirty baskets were auctioned and Fernie FC was in good financial shape for that season.[6]

With a charge of 25 cents for spectators, games were usually played Saturdays in the early evening. The host team was expected to honour the prevailing tradition in amateur sports at the time, namely the obligation to feed and accommodate the visiting team. It was an opportunity to act the gracious host, to display generosity and to smooth any feathers remaining ruffled after the game. Following a meal, the Saturday "smoker" usually involved speeches, recitations, and songs rendered by soloists from each team or by all assembled. The smoker often lasted well past midnight, with the host club certain to acknowledge the generosity of the local brewer or hotel for providing the beer and other leading merchants for sundries.

Of course, what mattered most to players and spectators alike happened on the field of play. Fernie FC expected to remain dominant in 1905. On Dominion Day, at a grand tournament held to contest for medals offered by District 18 of the United Mine Workers of America (UMWA), Fernie emerged with "the miners' medals" after a final victory over Coleman. Later in July, the club received another handsome medal for having defeated Cranbrook, and looked forward to a second CNPFL championship.[7] However, the appearance

Enjoying immediate success in 1905, the Coal Creek Football Club dominated during the early years of the CNPFL. Fernie & District Historical Society CNA 0127

of a new team did not augur well for Fernie. Coal Creek, having created its own sports field, formed a separate football club, enrolled in the CNPFL, and performed well at the Dominion Day tournament. With residency regulations in place, men living in Coal Creek were no longer eligible for membership in Fernie FC. The Coal Creek team, despite initial financial problems, went on to win the league championship, becoming the first holders of the silver cup donated by Fernie jeweller Albert Liphardt. The play of fullback Harry Allan, a former Scottish Internationalist, was widely regarded as the foundation of the team's success.[8]

It was the first of three league championships in a row for Coal Creek, but another prize—introduced at the start of the 1906 season—immediately became even more coveted than the Liphardt Cup. Albert Mutz of the Fort Steele Brewing Company donated what the *Fernie Free Press* described as "a beautiful challenge cup of very artistic design costing upwards of $100… to be played for by teams along the Crow between Pincher Creek and Cranbrook." Referred to variously as the Brewery Cup, the Fort Steele Brewing Company trophy and most commonly the Mutz Cup, its possession quickly emerged as the most prestigious honour in the world of Crowsnest Pass/Elk Valley football.[9]

Expecting to be in contention for league honours and the new challenge cup in 1906, the Fernie team reportedly began the season "with bright prospects," but ended it in last place. The CNPFL still boasted five members, but Blairmore and Pincher Creek were no longer among them. Football clubs in the Alberta Crowsnest had not rushed to join the fledgling league. Bellevue and Lundbreck had expressed interest, but Frank was the sole addition to the league in 1906. Only league-member clubs were eligible to contend for the Mutz Cup. When league play finally finished—a month later than initially scheduled due to several challenged results and disputes—cup play began.

As league champions, the formidable Coal Creek team also captured the miners' medals at the Dominion Day tournament at Fernie, and was widely expected to claim the new trophy. But Michel, which had only narrowly been edged out by Coal Creek in league competition, defeated "the Creekites" in an evening game played at Fernie. Presented with the Mutz Cup, the Michel team immediately marched through the streets of Fernie with their trophy held high. Spectators from Coal Creek and Michel had been well represented at the game, but gate receipts were disappointing according to the *Free Press*. The newspaper was critical of Fernie residents for their low turnout at the game, arguing: "Good sports advertises a town and adds considerably to its trade."[10]

Apart from the miners, community support for the local football club typically derived from merchants in general, and from brewers and hotel owners in particular. After Michel again upset Coal Creek to win the Mutz Cup in 1907, one hotel owner became very much involved in the CNPFL. Thomas Crahan, proprietor of the Michel Hotel and an investor in the Elk Valley Brewing Company, became president of Michel FC for what proved to be the very interesting season of 1908. It was the year Bellevue finally decided to join the league. It was also the year Hosmer joined, quickly earning league censure when two Hosmer players assaulted the referee in a match versus Coleman.[11] The massive fire at Fernie in August disrupted both league and cup schedules and undermined what had been hitherto a very good season for Fernie. When the club returned to the pitch, its final matches were played on the inferior football grounds at Coal Creek, where a distinct slope required the team winning the toss to decide whether to start the game playing uphill or downhill.

Most interesting about the 1908 season was the reversal of fortunes of the Coal Creek team, winless by the end of July and at the bottom of the league table. As the mighty had fallen, other teams could not fail to gloat a little. Following a 5–0 victory, Michel managed to have a five-stanza poem published in the *District Ledger*, noting with evident glee that Coal Creek retained only "a remnant of its former pride." Though its poetic merit is small, the first stanza effectively began the victory lap:

> They came with flags and ribbons gay,
> And laid big odds they'd win the day;
> But Michel boys played well and true,
> And learned Coal Creek a thing or two.[12]

No literary response from Coal Creek was recorded.

Whether on big odds or small, betting was an integral part of the local football experience. Money changed hands over such questions as who would score, which side would win, even who was most likely to have a fight. The league was aware it could not control spectators or even players on that score, but eventually was forced to adopt a formal regulation making clear that referees and linesmen were forbidden to bet on games in which they were actively participating. In 1908, the smart money was on Michel, which went on take both the league championship and the Mutz Cup.

Thomas Crahan may not have been a gambler, but he had a sense of where to place his money. In 1909, having become honorary league president, he donated $250 for the CNPFL to spend as it saw fit. It proved to be an embarrassment of riches. The appreciative league initially set aside $100 to be used for medals for members of the team winning the league competition, but could not decide how best to apportion the remaining funds. To address this unexpected problem, consideration was given to establishing a new cup. The general convention in competitive sport was that a team winning a cup three times in succession was entitled to its permanent possession. The Liphardt Cup, therefore, belonged to Coal Creek FC; as league champions of 1908, Michel FC had no trophy to show for it. The problem was resolved when Coal Creek magnanimously surrendered the Liphardt Cup to a grateful league executive, allowing postponement of a decision on how to spend the remainder of the Crahan donation.

Ever the hometown booster, the *District Ledger* published a photograph of the Fernie team in late September.[13] But again the honours went elsewhere. Coal Creek regained the league championship along with the Liphardt Cup in 1909 and Coleman captured its first Mutz Cup. Frank returned to the league after a year's absence, and, with the addition of Cowley for the first time, it appeared that the original aspiration to include communities as far eastward as Lethbridge was gaining some traction. Cowley quickly found it could not continue and in 1910 the geographic horizon shifted to the west. Well away from the Elk Valley, Cranbrook and Moyie could not qualify for league membership, but regulations pertaining to the Mutz Cup contained no such exclusion. Over the course of the season, teams from Coal Creek, Fernie and Michel travelled west, either to play friendlies against Cranbrook and Moyie, or, after Cranbrook eliminated Moyie, Mutz Cup playoff games against Cranbrook. It looked very much like the league was testing the possibility of a westward expansion in the near future.

The Michel Football Club photographed in front of the tipple bridge at Michel and under the crossbar of the goal in 1907. Fernie & District Historical Society FFP (07) 0066

The 1910 season is significant for another reason. Michel charged out of the gate, winning its first three matches with the contribution of a new player drawing considerable applause. Albert "Ginger" Goodwin made his first mark in British Columbia history not in the political arena, but rather on the football pitch. Along with Arthur Boothman and Tom Carney, Goodwin found employment with the Crow's Nest Pass Coal Company at Michel in April, just as the football club was preparing for the season. All three quickly won places on the team's forward line. In one game against Coal Creek in June, they gained individual recognition as both Goodwin and Boothman reportedly scored goals "in brilliant fashion."[14] The team stumbled later in the season and was eliminated from Mutz Cup play, but did hold on to win the league championship. Goodwin played in Michel's last league game in late September. At the same time, the mines at Michel went on short time, reducing opportunities for work. With the team's season apparently over, Goodwin and his Nova Scotian cohorts left Michel in early October with hopes of finding employment at Cumberland on Vancouver Island.[15]

They missed the chaotic conclusion to the season. Due to a combination of challenges, required replays and poor weather, the final game for the Mutz Cup was not played until mid-November in Fernie. Cranbrook, undefeated in the fourteen matches played that season, had long since qualified for the cup final and was no doubt surprised when Coleman—after an exceptionally poor season of league play—emerged as their opponent. The Cranbrook roster—by virtue of being comprised of railway men and sawmill workers—was a unique contender for a trophy hitherto held by teams of coal miners. The special train that brought the team to Fernie also included a number of women amongst the team's supporters, a sufficiently rare occurrence in the masculine culture of the CNPFL to elicit comment in the local newspapers.[16]

At Fernie, the hopeful players found November's football grounds covered with "lakes of water surrounding islands of mud." One observer, reporting on what he called "Mutz, mud and merriment," said the pitch strongly resembled "a sea of LePage's glue." The boisterous Coleman supporters who made the journey offered heavy odds on their team, counting on forward William Banks and his experience with both Kilmarnock and Manchester in the UK to make the difference. Despite the condition of the football pitch, both teams agreed to continue, but players and supporters must have realized from the start this was not a contest likely to be decided by skillful play. In a light snowfall and a developing south wind, the blue and white of Coleman eked out a 1–0 victory over the yellow and black of Cranbrook.[17]

And still, the football season continued. The league had belatedly decided to spend the rest of Thomas Crahan's gift on a new challenge trophy. The Crahan Cup—more splendid in appearance than the Liphardt and the Mutz—was to be awarded to the victor of what would henceforth be the marquee game of the season: a contest between the league champion and the Mutz winner. After nearly two months of inactivity and without the impressive forward line the team had relied upon all season, league champion Michel found itself back on the football pitch. The surprise perhaps is that they lost only by a score of 1–0. Against all odds, Coleman had managed to retain the Mutz and win

Each member of the league champion Michel football club received a medal in 1910. The medal above belonged to Albert "Ginger" Goodwin. Image courtesy Cumberland Museum and Archives

The Coleman Football Club captured the Mutz Cup in 1910. Crowsnest Museum and Archives CM-CO-284-01

the Crahan. The team returned home to a rousing welcome as "the undisputed champions of the Pass."[18]

Both the welcome given the conquering heroes and the newspaper coverage of the celebration are certainly indicative of civic pride, but with most (or, more likely, all) players being employees of the coal company, perhaps colliery pride is a more accurate description of the emotion felt by the cheering supporters. A victory by the miners of the International Coal and Coke Company of Coleman over the miners of the Crow's Nest Pass Coal Company of Michel was reason to celebrate the community of the workplace as much as the community of residence. The culture of shared identity, masculinity and solidarity—so strong amongst miners in the local workplace—was also fully embraced by members and supporters of the local football club. That culture was also extended to the junior teams that several clubs soon formed to encourage boys of up to eighteen years of age to participate in what was described as "healthy, manly sport."[19]

Drawing players and support almost entirely from the workforce of the local mine had other ramifications for a football club. Each season brought a few occasions when a team failed to show up for a scheduled match. This was often due to the mine manager offering an additional Saturday shift that could require some first-string players to go to work. The club then had to decide whether to send replacement players to the match or to save the expense involved by defaulting. The stark realities of the coal industry also meant that each season brought accidents in the mines. Benefit matches between clubs in adjacent communities were frequent and usually successful in raising funds for a disabled miner or the widow and family of a man killed.

Coleman FC, responsible for all the drama at the end the 1910 season, would be responsible for more of the same in 1911, but initially attention was focused elsewhere. Perhaps uncomfortable at the possibility of an expanded CNPFL including distant Cranbrook, teams on the Alberta side of the Pass formed a rival league in 1911. Blairmore FC—not a member of the CNPFL since its inaugural season—invited neighbouring communities to join it in a new Alberta-based league. Hillcrest, Lille, Lundbrek, Burmis, Bellevue and Passburg accepted the invitation to form what was variously called the Pass League, the Bellevue and District Football Association, and, confusingly, the Crow's Nest Pass Football League. The organization with the established claim to that name did not after all pursue a westward expansion, but was doubly surprised when Bellevue FC—apparently feeling strong and prosperous—registered in both leagues, while Fernie FC did not register at all.

The long-lasting coal strike of 1911 complicated league play, but did not prevent it. When out on strike, coal miners typically sought work locally either in forestry or with the railways, or farther afield as farm hands. Generally, the football clubs had sufficient members to fill in for absent players, but gate receipts declined as spectators tightened their purse strings. For Michel resident Sam Moores—a highly regarded member of the champion team of 1910—the strike brought a career change. The owner of the Grand Union Hotel in Coleman offered him a job at the hotel if he would move to Coleman and play for the local team. Moores accepted, never worked in a coal mine again, and was a mainstay of the Coleman team for many years.[20]

Cup play began earlier than usual in 1911 to avoid a repeat of the previous year's November mud match. By the end of a season largely free of challenges and disputes, Michel had repeated as league champion, Bellevue had captured its first Mutz Cup, and both looked forward to contesting for the Crahan trophy. However, to the dismay of Bellevue and Michel, and despite the fury of the league executive (which, of course, included its president—Thomas Crahan), Coleman refused to relinquish the prize. Coleman FC secretary Jonathan Graham, pointing to his broad experience on football executives in both England and the Crowsnest, insisted he had never heard of a club being called upon to relinquish a trophy without having an opportunity to defend it. Michel FC secretary J. Morris insisted football in the Pass "was doomed" if Graham's view prevailed. With the matter unresolved by the end of October, the cup remained in Coleman's hands, but only because there had been no game to contest for it.[21]

League and Trophy Winners of the CNPFL, 1904 to 1915			
	League	**Mutz Cup**	**Crahan Cup**
1904	Fernie	N/A	N/A
1905	Coal Creek	N/A	N/A
1906	Coal Creek	Michel	N/A
1907	Coal Creek	Michel	N/A
1908	Michel	Michel	N/A
1909	Coal Creek	Coleman	N/A
1910	Michel	Coleman	Coleman
1911	Michel	Bellevue	—
1912	Bellevue	Bellevue	Coleman
1913	Coal Creek	Coleman	Coleman
1914	—	Coal Creek	Frank
1915	—	—	—

Coleman registered with the rival Pass League in 1912, as did Blairmore and Hillcrest. In its second season, that organization had acquired a cup donated by Burns and Co. and a new name—the Southern Alberta Football League. Fernie FC reorganized, and, with the promised backing of practically the entire local business community, announced it would return to league and cup play.[22] With Fernie back in the CNPFL and Hosmer seriously thinking about rejoining, football in the region seemed to be moving toward a division determined by the provincial border. However, with decisions that then caused much early-season confusion, Bellevue stuck with the CNPFL, while Coleman ultimately registered with both leagues.

At the second organizational meeting of the CNPFL for the year, Coleman brought a proposal to the table that resulted in further confusion. Through the auspices of Coleman FC, the Calgary Brewing Company offered the league a new silver trophy. Not the kind of offer that can be politely declined, it meant that the CNPFL would become an organization with an embarrassment of silverware for just five member clubs. A complete restructuring was adopted. The Calgary Brewing Company Cup—even more ornate than the Crahan—became the new trophy signifying league championship, replacing the Liphardt Cup, which became the prize played for by the league's emerging junior teams. At the same time, the CNPFL satisfied Coleman by confirming that only league members could play for the Mutz trophy, while competition for the Crahan Cup would be open to any football club in the Crowsnest/Elk Valley region.[23]

With the complexities of trophy matters settled, the season progressed along the lines of its predecessors, with all the usual impediments and complications along the way. Hosmer joined at the last minute, requiring a rearrangement of league fixtures. For the first time, the use of goal nets became mandatory. A foot of snow meant the cancellation of several matches in mid-June. Basket socials continued to raise funds and smokers continued to provide enjoyment for players after hostilities had ceased on the football pitch. For example, following one match, host club Bellevue gave "a smoker and social" in the Socialist Hall, where two ten-gallon kegs of beer were rolled in by the proprietor of the Southern Hotel, songs were sung by members of each team, speeches described the virtues of the teams, and the referee was complimented on the way he had conducted the game.[24] Less collegially, predictable challenges again prolonged the season. Bellevue finally emerged as the first winner of the Calgary Brewing Company Cup after a close match with Michel, the result of which was immediately but unsuccessfully contested. Bellevue also took home the Mutz Cup, and after a surprising challenge by Hosmer—last place finisher in league play—Coleman retained the Crahan Cup.

The 1913 season began with optimism tempered by an old headache. The Hillcrest Football Club raised over $200 through a basket social and dance, and decided to abandon the Southern Alberta Football League in favour of the CNPFL.[25] Blairmore FC made the same decision. It was Coleman again that presented the headache. Insisting that, after three years, the Crahan Cup had found a permanent home, Coleman was faced with expulsion from the league after refusing several requests to surrender it. The league claimed that—following the example set by Coal Creek in returning the Liphardt Cup in 1909— all trophies were league property. At the last minute, Coleman FC secretary Jonathan Graham made "satisfactory arrangements," and the CNPFL announced the season's fixtures for eight teams. For the first time, the

Anthony Carter faced many challenges as secretary of the CNPFL. Fernie & District Historical Society DL-PF-1909-00294

league published its complete rules and regulations, most of which were unchanged from previous years. All matches were to be played under the Football Association's International Board Rules. Clubs paid a $20 league membership fee; referees were to be paid $4 per game plus travelling and accommodation expenses; and home teams were to be responsible for meals and accommodation for fourteen members of visiting teams.[26]

The executive officers elected for the year dispelled any doubts yet remaining that the CNPFL was a miners' league. The president was Coleman miner Joseph Grafton, the honorary vice-presidents were all managers of the region's collieries, and the new secretary, Anthony Carter, was also secretary of UMWA District 18. As a resident of Fernie, Carter had easy access to the *District Ledger*, and the full weekly reports the newspaper printed for most of the season were submitted by him. Several clubs reported successful smokers and basket socials, but successful fundraising did not necessarily translate to success on the pitch. In good financial shape and with a change of club colours from blue and white to green and white,

Fernie's early season performance was woeful nevertheless. A complete reorganization of the club's executive took place in late June. Fernie then walloped the equally woeful Blairmore team by a score of 8–1, Blairmore quitting the league soon after.

The top of the league table was very tight with Bellevue, Coleman and Coal Creek contesting for the Calgary Brewing Company Cup. At season's end, Coal Creek emerged with its first league title since 1909 and club supporters were eagerly anticipating the Mutz Cup final against Coleman in Blairmore on Saturday, September 20. Coal Creek could always count on community support. On game day, approximately two hundred spectators joined the team on the 7:45 train to Fernie, then rushed to collect their weekly wages at the pay box by the coke ovens before hurrying to catch the specially arranged CPR train to Blairmore. After several hours of anticipation and celebration alongside equally enthusiastic Coleman supporters, the scoreless draw that followed was profoundly disappointing. Under CNPFL rules, a replay was required and the league executive immediately declared it would take place at Blairmore on the following Wednesday.[27]

Defeated in cup play, Coal Creek could still boast of winning the league championship in 1913. Image of team member John Manning's medal courtesy of Ronald Greene

Even by CNPFL standards, the brouhaha that followed was exceptional. The decision to replay at Blairmore was quickly overturned. Coal Creek had objected to having to travel so far again, and formally requested the game be played on the grounds at Fernie. In support of that position, the manager of the Fernie-Fort Steele Brewing Company wrote to league secretary Anthony Carter to complain that a prize given by a Fernie business should not be played for in Alberta. He declared that Albert Mutz donated the trophy on the understanding that the final game would always be played at Coal Creek or Fernie. A letter writer signing as "Sport Follower" accused Carter of caving in to pressure from his friends at Coal Creek; Carter replied he had no vote in the decision made by the league executive not to replay at Blairmore. Sport Follower returned to the fray, repeated his accusations and mocked the notion that the Mutz Cup should be contested only on football grounds located in British Columbia. As a final word, the editor of the *District Ledger* regretted the annual "repetition of this bickering and quarrelling" and declared he would publish no further correspondence on the matter.[28]

The final game was first postponed to October 4 with a location to be decided, and finally to October 11 at Michel. When all was said and done, before a small crowd braving poor weather, Coal Creek fell 2–0 to Coleman in the final Mutz Cup game, and a week later were defeated in the Crahan Cup final—again by Coleman and again at Michel. For Coleman, capturing both trophies revived memories of the triumphs of 1910. A large crowd and the town band greeted the evening train when the team arrived home with the Crahan Cup in hand once more. It must have seemed like the trophy had found its natural home.[29]

In late March 1914, CNPFL delegates meeting at the King Edward Hotel in Fernie were pleased to hear of a modest operating surplus. In pursuit of a more respectable image, businessmen and civic politicians were added to the roster of honorary vice-presidents. From Fernie alone came Crow's Nest Pass Coal Company manager William Wilson, Mayor Jonathan Gates, brewer Albert Mutz, and store owners Amos Trites and Roland Wood.[30] Following a lengthy discussion on policies, it was agreed that drastic changes—also in pursuit of respectability—were needed in "conducting the affairs of the league." Henceforth, contentious matters would not be placed before the whole executive, as in previous years, but before the president, vice-president and secretary only. Their decisions were to be final. It was a process that would soon be put to the test.

It was another year of expansion. At the second executive meeting, secretary Carter urged the acceptance of a late application from Corbin FC to join the league. Some delegates noted that train connections to Corbin were poor and expressed concern about the community's ability to finance a team, but the application was accepted and a new schedule was hurriedly drawn up to include nine teams. From the Alberta side of the Pass, Coleman, Hillcrest and Bellevue were joined by Frank, particularly proud to return to league play after an absence of two years. A brass band was present at its opening game, and the basket social, dinner and dance sponsored by Frank FC a week later was well supported. Comparable fundraising events were held by all clubs as each viewed the new season with a fresh measure of optimism. Coal Creek FC was particularly keen, boasting its brand-new football grounds would be "the best ground in the Pass."[31] There were indications, however, that the continuing economic depression was having an effect. The dinner and dance organized by Hillcrest FC raised barely enough money to cover expenses.[32]

Once organized and ready for the CNPFL season, clubs were required by secretary Carter to submit the names of all registered players. Along with the names of referees and club secretaries, club membership lists were published in full by the *District Ledger* at the end of May.[33] The lists reveal apparently healthy, vibrant member clubs and a league confident of its future. The lists also reveal that football in the Crowsnest/Elk Valley was an entirely British affair. Of the more than two hundred surnames found in these lists, only one is recognizable as being of non-British origin. Miner-based football clubs cannot readily be seen as bastions of privilege, but they certainly were bastions of British cultural identity, outposts of Empire in a foreign land. In a region where barely half the residents were of British origin, where Italian and Slav immigrants were employed in all the mines, membership of football clubs reveals a clear and profound social gulf between immigrant groups. Even a full decade after the first football clubs were formed, the British coal miners of the CNPFL were keeping the game entirely to themselves.[34]

In that respect, the football clubs mirrored the leadership— though not the membership—of UMWA District 18, where local union executives and the district executive also remained predominantly British. The clubs also mirrored the willingness of individual local unions to disregard decisions of the parent organization when their concerns were perceived as more important. As secretary of District 18, Anthony Carter was familiar with the difficulty of dealing with restless local unions; as secretary of the CNPFL, of course, he was well aware that Coleman FC had frequently demonstrated the tendency to deny the authority of the league. But he could not have predicted that Frank FC would become the focus of dissent for the 1914 season.

At the first match of the season between Frank and Hillcrest in early May, which attracted as many as five hundred spectators and a brass band, two players were sent off for fighting. Eager to assert a stronger hand in matters of discipline, the league quickly imposed two-week suspensions on the pair. If the message was intended to be heard across the league, it was not received at Coal Creek. The match versus Frank on the new football grounds there later in May resulted in a controversy that would undermine the league until the end of the season. Unhappy with the referee throughout, Coal Creek players and supporters became incensed at the awarding of a questionable goal that gave Frank the lead early in the second half. A brawl resulted. Spectators invaded the pitch, and the referee—fearing for his safety—left the field.

Along with witnesses, the unfortunate referee was summoned to appear at a league meeting at Frank a few days later. Mindful that the situation was a repeat of a match at Coal Creek the previous season (when spectators invaded the pitch during a similar donnybrook to kick at visiting Hosmer players), and determined to live up to the promise of improved conduct, wide-ranging measures were imposed. Broadly speaking, they were intended to protect referees and to encourage decorum by players and spectators. One Coal Creek player was given a month's suspension; a replay was ordered, but not at Coal Creek, which had its new grounds suspended for the season; Coal Creek was ordered to pay expenses to the referee and to Frank for hotel and travel costs that would result from the replay. Coal Creek FC howled in protest but accepted the decisions; Frank FC insisted the victory was theirs and adamantly refused to accept the decision requiring a replay.[35]

One further decision made at that meeting created another problem for the remainder of the season: the referee was found deficient and his resignation was demanded. Many found that demand distressing. Typically dressed in a working man's three-piece suit and cap, the referee for any given match represented the authority of the CNPFL. The league had taken great pains to ensure each game was refereed by an individual of solid reputation who was neither a resident of the host community nor that of the visiting team. In the absence of a league-appointed referee at a scheduled game, the two sides would have to find a replacement agreeable to each—not always an easy task for clubs that so frequently agreed on so little.

The controversial game and its aftermath drew attention from beyond football circles and the columns of the *District Ledger*. Fernie's chief newspaper, the *Free Press*, had long since acknowledged that Association Football was "the miner's favourite game," but it was not

The Hillcrest Football Club, 1914. (* killed in the Hillcrest disaster) **Back row:** Frank Bostock*, M. Dickenson*, W. Rochester*, Thomas Dugdale, W. Miller*, possibly Joseph Brehler, R. Dugdale*, H. Jepson, Mr. Fisher, John Moorhouse. **Front row:** W.G. Miller,* Jock Dugdale, H. Varley, W. Kyle, Wm. Fines*. Crowsnest Museum and Archives CM-HM-09-05

a sport favoured by its editor, John Wallace. His personal preferences—baseball, lacrosse, curling and shooting—all received much more comprehensive coverage. The *Free Press* rarely mentioned the league or the sport, but chose this moment to make a substantial comment on the game of football for the first time in nearly four years. Following a Dominion Day tournament involving teams from Fernie, Coal Creek and Corbin, Wallace noted: "These games were enlivened by a few fistic encounters, which seems to be the sole reason why the game is tolerated by the crowd."[36] This was certainly not an indication that greater respectability for the sport was being achieved.

Other problems were accumulating. A decade of prosperity in the coal industry was over and the financial concerns of member clubs were increasing. League stalwart Bellevue officially withdrew from play in early June, while Hosmer was forced to withdraw when the Canadian Pacific Railway Company announced the immediate termination of its Elk Valley coal operation in late June. But far worse news had already shaken coal communities throughout the region. On June 19, an explosion at the Hillcrest mine killed 189 men. The sheer scale of the disaster shocked residents already far too familiar with loss of life in local coal mines. Football rivalries were suddenly the furthest thing from anyone's mind. All league games scheduled for June 20 were cancelled. Two members of the Hillcrest team on shift that morning survived the disaster, but eleven of the club members listed in the *District Ledger* three weeks earlier lost their lives. Robert Petrie of Frank FC was also killed.[37] Clearly, Hillcrest could not continue in league play.

Several benefit matches by remaining teams were played throughout the Pass to raise money for the Hillcrest Relief Fund as the league tried to reorganize the schedule to resume the season. At an executive meeting at the end of July, Frank restated its refusal to accept the judgment about the Coal Creek game. But it didn't matter. Grappling with a growing number of defaulted games, the executive at the same meeting made the decision to abandon league play for the rest of the season. Michel then withdrew from cup competitions. At the same time, as the challenge cups became the focus of attention much earlier than usual, two veteran referees—perhaps still unhappy at the treatment of their colleague in May—declared they would not fulfill their cup obligations.[38]

The league waived residency requirements for clubs affected by the Hillcrest disaster. Harry Jepson, a registered member of Hillcrest FC, was permitted to play for Frank in cup play, and, with the addition of several players from Bellevue, Hillcrest was able to fulfill its cup tie commitments. The hybrid Hillcrest-Bellevue squad fell to Coal Creek, which set up a final Mutz Cup tie between Coal Creek and Frank at Fernie in mid-August. Just as had occurred the previous year, a large contingent from Coal Creek—99 percent of the population, according to one hyperbolic commentator—caught the train to Fernie, but just like the previous year, they were disappointed with an inconclusive draw. Frank had to return to Fernie a few days later to meet defeat before a much smaller crowd. Fernie mayor Jonathan Gates commended the Frank players on their sportsmanlike willingness to travel to Fernie twice in one week. He then handed the Mutz Cup to the Coal Creek team, triumphant in cup play for the first time in its history.[39]

Although the Corbin team had been described as "a treat to witness" in June, observers were nevertheless surprised to see Coal Creek eliminated by Corbin for the Crahan Cup. On the other hand, Frank's qualification for the cup final surprised no one. Both Corbin and Frank had performed well all season and the Crahan Cup tie in Hillcrest just before Labour Day promised to be what the CNPFL needed badly—a clean game of high-quality competition. The match lived up to expectations as Frank claimed the first trophy in the club's history. Both teams then attended an evening dance at the Frank Hotel with the Crahan Cup on display.[40] Despite the celebrations, however, it was clear to all that the 1914 CNPFL season had staggered to its conclusion.

Attempts to prepare for the 1915 season were not much more encouraging. The initial meeting of the league at Fernie in April accomplished little. An executive was elected, but the creation of a schedule was postponed to its second meeting in Michel on May 8. The usual early season optimism is missing from fragmentary reports in the *District Ledger* and the several newspapers of the Pass. Wartime financial demands were placing increasingly heavy burdens on individuals, businesses and organizations. Amongst others, appeals from the Red Cross, for Belgian relief and for the Patriotic Fund were escalating. The economic depression continued and the mines were still operating only part time. Business owners were less able to subscribe to the local football club; individuals were less likely to afford a ticket to a basket social or even to a local match; military manpower demands

Frank Football Club with Crahan Cup, 1914. Crowsnest Museum and Archives CM-FR-284-01

were drawing heavily upon miners throughout the entire region. The CNPFL shrunk again to just five clubs. To reduce travel and associated costs, the league decided on a new structure. Alberta teams would play each other exclusively, as would teams from British Columbia. The winner of each division would meet to decide a league champion at Michel on July 3.

Having made that decision, and presumably having to reduce its own costs, the league announced it would not meet again until the day of the championship game, again at Michel. In sharp contrast to the previous two years, league secretary Anthony Carter submitted no reports to the *District Ledger*. Some results do however appear in the weekly reports of local union correspondents, most consistently from Coal Creek and Coleman. What little enthusiasm remained seemed to be concentrated in Coal Creek. The only successful fundraiser mentioned in the newspapers of 1915 was held there in April, and the new football grounds, now called Victoria Park, was no longer under suspension. The only recorded complaint also emanated from Coal Creek. When Michel failed to show up for a scheduled match in June, the correspondent noted that Coal Creek FC had "practically depleted their treasury" by travelling to Michel earlier in the season. Apparently Michel FC had no such store of funds at its command by the midpoint of the season.

The nearly empty football grounds at Michel, *circa* 1915. Fernie & District Historical Society 4818do

A century on, the Crahan Cup today is just a little worse for wear. Image courtesy Fernie Museum and Archives FM.2022.6.3

There was none of the usual gloating about victories by local correspondents to the *District Ledger*, suggesting scheduled games were not being played. Coal Creek and Coleman emerged as respective champions of their provincial divisions, but whether a final match between them was played is not recorded. The final newspaper comment about football for 1915 reveals only disappointment. Noting that a meeting of the league occurred at Michel on July 10—a week later than originally scheduled—the correspondent from Coal Creek wrote: "The leather chasers and enthusiasts are somewhat disappointed at the turn of events." Whatever the specifics of that turn of events were, for the second year in a row league play was not completed; for the first time, neither the Mutz nor the Crahan were contested. Due to a combination of local circumstances, the CNPFL echoed the decision taken by the Football Association in England, suspending play for the duration of the war.

A significant chapter in local sports history had ended with barely a whimper. After its tentative beginning in 1904, the CNPFL was an integral part of life in the coal-mining communities of the Elk Valley and Crowsnest Pass. Although their membership revealed class and ethnic divisions, the football clubs were symbols of civic pride. The names of a few stellar players—Allan, Banks, Goodwin, Boothman—are recorded in a few newspaper reports, but the names of most players (stellar or otherwise) are irretrievably lost in time. Perennial disputes and quarrels amongst member clubs tested the patience of league officials both on and off the pitch. Internal squabbling, a weak local economy and the demands of the war in Europe brought collapse. Once gone, the CNPFL was sorely missed. Many wondered if such a league could ever return.

Postscript

The end of the Great War brought attempts by individuals and organizations to re-create the world they had lost after 1914. Local football was no exception, but changes were afoot. Near the war's end, a team from Blairmore composed entirely of British players played a team from Frank composed entirely of Slavs. By May 1920, the Crow's Nest Pass Football League was back on its feet, with team rosters that were beginning to reflect the ethnic diversity of the region. Yet there were distinct echoes of the pre-war game. Arnold Varley, a member of the Hillcrest team of 1914—after service in France with the 192nd Crow's Nest Pass Battalion—returned to the football pitch, suffered an injury and was unable to work. A match was arranged to raise funds for his benefit. And, reviving memories of earlier triumphs, Coleman won the first post-war Mutz Cup.

There were other lingering echoes from the pre-war game, one in particular coming from up the narrow valley leading to Coal Creek. On August 13, 1915, just over a month after the suspension of play by the CNPFL, Andrew Cairns of the Coal Creek football team walked into the recruiting office of the 54th Kootenay Battalion in Fernie and enlisted. Three days later, fellow players William Newbery and James Wilson did the same. Eight more members of Coal Creek enlisted by the end of August, prompting the *Fernie Free Press* to note that the team had "enlisted in a body." Perhaps knowingly, perhaps unknowingly, the Coal Creek football team had followed the example of Heart of Midlothian, the premier Scottish team famous for enlisting all together in November 1914. Seven Hearts players lost their lives in the war. From the Coal Creek football team, so too did John Myers, Thomas Walker and Thomas Martin.

From Beirut and Damascus

Syrian Merchants
in the Elk Valley

It must now be impossible to be unaware that years of civil wars in Syria have resulted in immeasurable suffering and distressingly high numbers of casualties and refugees. In British Columbia, almost every community now includes residents who are Syrian-born. A century ago, that was certainly not the case. According to census information, there were then approximately only one hundred people of Syrian origin resident in British Columbia, the majority of them living in the greater Vancouver area. Surprisingly, Fernie was home to most of the rest.

That fact certainly came as a surprise to me. While conducting research about life in Fernie during the years of the Great War, I learned that a merchant of Syrian origin and his family were well established in the community. After *Fernie at War* was published, I found there was a second such merchant, and then found reference to a third and a fourth. Chastened but intrigued, I thought I might look at census records, business directories and newspapers to learn what I could about these businessmen. These sources indicate that no fewer than seven merchant families and a number of other individuals of Syrian origin were living and working in Fernie during the war years.

The Syrians who found their way to the Elk Valley were from what was then known as Assyria, a province of the Ottoman Empire that included Lebanon. Typically, they had established themselves first in eastern Canada or the eastern United States before joining the broad movement of population westwards during the Laurier years. With the opening of the mines at Coal Creek, Fernie became an instant town, attracting entrepreneurs hopeful of providing goods and services to the Crow's Nest Pass Coal Company and its employees. There appears to be no reference to Syrian business activity during the earliest years at Fernie, but, at nearby Morrissey Mines, one of the first businesses to open its doors was a general store operated by brothers Ayoub and Nassif Kfoury.

Conflicting information about the Kfoury brothers is found in census returns, but it is clear they were not recent immigrants to Canada. Born in Damascus, Nassif Kfoury and his wife had moved to Montreal perhaps as early as 1889, Nassif working as a travelling salesman. His brother Ayoub soon followed, and, by the turn of the century, his two daughters and elderly mother had joined them. It seems that most members of the Kfoury family remained in Quebec while the venture west was being tested by Nassif and Ayoub.

First included in *Henderson's British Columbia Gazetteer and Directory* in 1904, their store at Morrissey was likely first established in 1903. In April 1904 Nassif's wife, an adult sister and three children arrived in Morrissey to take up residence above the store, which was located opposite the Alexandra Hotel.[41] The death of one of those children soon afterwards and ongoing problems with the local mines soon encouraged the brothers to set long-term sights elsewhere. Nearby Fernie provided an attractive and accessible alternative. The economy there was booming, but other well-established businesses offered the merchandise typical of a general store, and another hopeful Syrian merchant, Michael Boassaly, was also interested in Fernie. Nonetheless, Ayoub and Nassif saw a niche for dry goods, footwear and fine Turkish tobacco. They first established a store in Fernie sometime during 1905.[42] With a slight change of spelling in their surname and weekly advertisements in the *District Ledger*, the Kefoury brothers opened more permanently in rented premises next to the Bank of Commerce on Victoria Avenue in July 1906. They cannot have been too pleased that Boassaly was in business at a temporary location that summer opposite the coke ovens and was stocking precisely the same merchandise.[43] They were likely much more pleased by the marriage of their sister Mary to fellow Syrian Asouph Haddad, who had recently moved to Fernie from Brandon to set up his own business.

The optimism of all residents of Fernie received a sharp setback with the great fire of August 1908. Seeing their store and all its stock destroyed by the great fire would have been discouraging indeed for Nassif and Ayoub Kefoury. They were back in business in a temporary building by early October, only to lose $100 to an armed robber a week

KEFOURY BROTHERS

Jewelery, Clothing and Outfitting

Wholesale and Retail Merchants

Specialty, Watches, Notions, Fancy Goods

Established Six Years   · · ·   FERNIE, B. C.

Advertisement in *Progressive Fernie*, 1909. Fernie & District Historical Society DL-PF-1909-0062

later.[44] However, the dynamic reconstruction of the city convinced them to stay, and in July 1909 they demonstrated their intention to be part of Fernie's rebirth. Purchasing a property on Victoria Avenue between the Northern Hotel and the Henderson Block, they undertook to erect a two-storey building to serve as their residence and permanent business location.[45]

The new Fernie rising from the ashes of the old apparently appealed to Syrian-born merchants far and wide. By the time the 1911 census was conducted, six more Syrian families had come to settle in Fernie. The family heads are almost all identified as pedlars or merchants. George Yohnis had gone initially to the United States before moving to Canada in 1909; he would support his young family as a seller of general merchandise in Fernie for over a decade. Khalil Ghiz was also a pedlar, while his son found work at the sawmill. Another pedlar—the name is illegible in the census return—was a very recent arrival, with one infant having been born in Syria and another born in British Columbia. Frank Kefoury—perhaps related to Ayoub and Nassif—moved his large American-born family to Fernie after nearly two decades in Alaska.[46]

Two other families—Rahal and Haddad—were also beginning local careers that would soon make them as well known as the Kefoury brothers. The Rahal family followed a path similar to that of the Kefourys—arriving in eastern Canada in the late 1800s, and then moving westwards. Census records indicate that three Rahal brothers arrived in Fernie around 1909–1910. The eldest, Nicholas Rahal, established himself as a merchant of clothing and dry goods in Fernie, while Edward and the youngest brother, John, opened a dry goods and grocery store in Hosmer.[47] With prospects of their sons apparently filled with promise, parents Ferris and Sadie Rahal soon joined Nicholas and his family on Howland Avenue in Fernie.

Positive reports from Asouph Haddad persuaded his brothers, Abraham and William, that Fernie offered opportunities. All three were more recent immigrants than were members of the Kefoury and Rahal families, having arrived in Canada only around 1903. Four more Haddad brothers—perhaps relatives, perhaps just sharing a surname—also arrived in Fernie soon after the fire. As the Haddad Brothers, James and Norman opened for business as the first tenant in one of the storefronts in the still unfinished Miners' Union Building in March 1909, offering dry goods and men's clothing.[48] Another brother, Edward, is identified as a local businessman (probably in connection with the store), but only in newspaper reports; a fourth brother, Roger, was a mill worker according to the census of 1911.[49]

One of the most notable new residents of the community was the Kefoury brothers' elderly mother, Arnfly, who moved from Quebec to join her family in Fernie soon after Ayoub and Nassif decided to construct their permanent building. Her arrival sent tongues a-wagging. Short in stature, dressed always in black, ninety-six years old at the time of her arrival in Fernie, practically blind and usually carrying a stick to help with mobility, she must have surprised anyone seeing her for the first time. In a small community where stories about "the evil eye" were widely believed, her appearance and glance askew apparently gave young children abundant cause to frighten themselves with imagined stories. Her reported ability to carry a hundred-pound sack of coal on her back only added to youthful speculation about her secret powers.[50]

Even as the local economy suffered a sharp reversal, more Syrian immigrants were arriving. Pedlar Khalil Saad and dry goods merchant Harry Joseph are found in the census of 1911. By the eve of the Great War, Khalil Saad was in business at 315 Victoria Avenue. Working with him was Joseph Saad—perhaps a brother, certainly a relative. Jeffries and Co.'s *Southeast Kootenay Directory* of 1914 also indicates that Albert and Lena Joseph had recently arrived from the United States and that John Ameer was operating a business in conjunction with the Palace Drug Store.[51]

As the more established Syrian merchant families knew well, other small businesses in Fernie and the grand Trites-Wood store all offered comparable merchandise. In such a crowded field, several Syrian merchants began to turn their attention elsewhere. None of them apparently saw opportunity at Michel or Natal. Their favoured destinations were the coal communities of Alberta's Crowsnest Pass. The first to consider relocating were the Haddad brothers, who dissolved their partnership in April 1910. James apparently liked his prospects in Bellevue, where he and Roger initially opened a general store and would later add a gas station. Frank Kefoury relocated his large family to operate the Blairmore Trading Company; Albert and Lena Joseph established a similar business at Hillcrest. Edward Rahal transferred his Cash Grocery to Blairmore after mining operations at Hosmer were abruptly ended in 1914, and he suffered losses estimated at $4,000.[52]

Sharing a surname does not necessarily mean family connections, but if the Syrian merchant families were not related before they immigrated, they certainly became so in British Columbia. The Kefoury, Haddad and Rahal families were all connected through marriages recorded at Fernie. Of course, not all marriages are made in heaven. Just before Haboba Rahal died in the Fernie hospital in 1913, she alleged mistreatment at the hands of her estranged husband. Nicholas Rahal quickly found himself in the city jail charged with murder. At the subsequent trial, when the attending doctor declared there were no physical indications of abuse and friends and relatives all testified they had witnessed none, the charge against the accused was dismissed. The case received widespread publicity both locally and provincially, attention that no immigrant community would welcome.[53]

In the summer of 1914—probably combining personal and business reasons—James Haddad and his uncle Frank Kefoury travelled together to Assyria. Their timing was poor and the visit was complicated by the outbreak of war in Europe. Although the Ottoman Empire was not yet a declared belligerent, general mobilization was ordered there in early August and able-bodied men were required to be ready for military service. James and his uncle had to bribe officials in order to obtain the false passports needed for a return journey to Canada in October 1914.[54]

Amongst the Syrians remaining in Fernie was Abraham Haddad, and, just before Christmas 1914, he rented the storefront of the Miners' Union Building recently vacated by the Fernie branch of the Socialist Party of Canada. It was a brave decision as Fernie was in

Unidentified men with the Grand and Haddad signs in the background, *circa* 1915–1920. Fernie & District Historical Society 3920do

the depths of a prolonged economic depression. Described as a "clothing and notions merchant," Haddad offered stationery, suits, rubber boots and jewellery, some of which merchandise was carted away by thieves just a few weeks after the store opened. The robbery was part of a crime spree that was finally ended in March 1915 when the thieves were arrested in the Annex neighbourhood and some of the merchandise recovered.[55]

Fitting into the resource-frontier society of Fernie cannot have been easy, especially for older family members who spoke little or no English. Apart from advertisements appearing in local newspapers, references in local historical records to members of the merchant families from Syria are few. Yet those few references do indicate a process of adaptation to the host society. Donations to community fundraising drives and to the Patriotic Fund, as well as purchases of Victory Bonds by members of all the Syrian families, are recorded during the war years.[56] After the war, a daughter of Frank Kefoury played for the Coleman Shamrocks against the Fernie Swastikas. Even Nassif Kefoury's conviction for operating an illegal still in the Fernie Annex during the prohibition period — an activity widely shared in the region at the time — suggests a certain accommodation to local standards.[57]

The years following the end of the Great War were not prosperous ones in the Elk Valley and Crowsnest Pass, and businesses had to adapt to survive. Members of the Haddad and Kefoury families entered into a partnership, advertising jointly for a retail salesman in May 1919 and contributing to Fernie's Dominion Sports Day as the Kefoury-Haddad Company.[58] Independently, Abraham Haddad left the Miners' Union Building to lease the former McLean Drug Store space on Victoria Avenue, and then decided to erect his own building opposite the King Edward Hotel on corner lots purchased from Amos Trites in September 1919. At that location, he opened the Golden Lion Trading Company, offering for sale everything from Singer sewing machines to shoes and lightbulbs. For others, the Crowsnest communities continued to appeal. Both Khalil and Joseph Saad decided the future looked brighter in Alberta. Khalil purchased the Haddad brothers' Bellevue store in June 1920, and, in October, Joseph acquired the store in Blairmore from Edward Rahal. The Saad families then left Fernie for their respective Crowsnest communities.[59]

Wherever they lived in the region, Syrian merchant families would have followed the treaty-making process in Paris with great interest. By the Treaty of Sèvres in 1920, their birthplaces were no longer within Ottoman territory, but were all located in the French-mandated territories of Lebanon and Syria. Curiosity may have been sufficiently strong to tempt some to return — at least for a visit. At the same time, the post-war economic downturn in Fernie was having an effect. George Yohnis closed his dry-goods business and declared he was returning to Syria.[60] Abraham Haddad sold the Golden Lion Trading Company and moved to Cranbrook in 1923. The Kefoury family, too, soon withdrew from the region. Leaving Ayoub to run the store, Nassif — in failing health — moved to Vancouver along with his mother, Arnfly.[61] Ayoub briefly went into partnership with John Rahal, who by then had worked as a sales clerk for Kefoury Brothers for several years. However, in 1924, the name Kefoury — for the first time in two decades — was no longer included in business listings of the Elk Valley.

Individual members of the merchant families Yohnis, Kefoury

and Haddad may have remained in Fernie after the departure of the heads of families. The soon-to-be-released census of 1931 should provide some information on that point. But it was the Rahal family name alone that remained to carry on the mercantile tradition of the Syrians of Fernie. At the age of just thirteen, John Rahal had been a salesman in the family grocery store at Hosmer in 1911; still a young man, he took over the Kefoury operation with older brother Nicholas as a partner when the Kefourys left town. For two decades, Fernie residents were familiar with the Rahal Brothers store.

John Rahal in front of his store.
Fernie & District Historical Society 0207

Following the death of Nicholas in 1947, with just a change of name, the Jonathan Rahal store continued to offer a wide range of goods and souvenirs to the local community until the 1980s.

Postscript

The Syrian residents of a century ago were not refugees fleeing war-torn regions of the Middle East. Like millions of others, they were economic migrants hoping to find a better life in the young country called Canada. Whether or not and to what extent those hopes were realized is perhaps a question only their descendants—in the Elk Valley, the Crowsnest and elsewhere—can truly answer. With the passage of more than a century since the first hopeful arrivals in the region, even descendants may be hard-pressed to explain why Fernie then seemed such a beacon of promise for immigrant businessmen from the Assyrian province of the Ottoman Empire.

John Rahal, the community's last Syrian-born merchant, died in Fernie in 1968.

On Stage Tonight

Jeanne Russell and
Boris Karloff in Fernie

The debut performance by the Jeanne Russell Company in Fernie on the evening of November 25, 1909, was anticipated with enthusiasm by the citizens of Fernie. Indeed, many felt an obligation to attend. They were aware that very soon after Fernie burned on the first day of August 1908, the Jeanne Russell Company—then performing in Edmonton—organized a benefit performance that raised $700 for victims of the disaster. Jeanne Russell had contributed personally. And now, here they were, the entire repertory company booked as one of the first acts to appear at the recently opened Miners' Union Theatre.

Though well known to western Canadian audiences in the pre-war years, Jeanne Russell and the performers in her touring group are names familiar now only to the most serious of theatre historians. Russell and her husband, Ray Brandon, both hailed from Utah, where they met as performers in a local theatre in 1906. Following the lead of a family member who moved to Edmonton, Brandon and Russell formed the Jeanne Russell Company there as the repertory troupe for the Dominion Theatre in June 1908. It was at the Dominion, just over a month later, that the fundraiser was held for the victims of the Fernie fire.[62]

The *District Ledger* newspaper reminded its readers of the fundraiser and expressed high expectations of the scheduled performance. The troupe certainly looked impressive in the promotional content appearing in the Fernie newspapers. In one advertisement, the caption to a full-length photograph of Jeanne Russell mentioned her "New York Company"; in another, she was described as "Canada's Greatest Favourite." Although such claims willfully ignored the company's Utah/Alberta roots, the hyperbole proved immaterial when

Just in time for the Russell troupe's first performance, these chairs were replaced by permanent seating. Fernie & District Historical Society DL-PF-1909-0271

the performance of the comedy *Cousin Kate* drew a packed house. The reviews were uniformly positive. Sets were admired as precise replications of those introduced by Ethel Barrymore at the play's debut in New York; the performance was described as the greatest "dramatic event of the season," and Russell was applauded as "an artist of quite exceptional power."[63]

From the other side of the lights, what members of the theatre troupe thought of their first visit to Fernie went unrecorded, but they must have found it rather peculiar. November 25 was a provincial election day in British Columbia, and the management of the Miners' Union Theatre was concerned that interest in the election could negatively affect box office receipts. To persuade the politically oriented to attend, advertisements promised full returns would be received by wire and made available to the audience. This was likely the first and only occasion the Jeanne Russell Company had to share the bill with the periodic announcement of election results.

Advertisements from the *Fernie Free Press* of November 26, 1909.

Theatre management need not have worried. The performance of the play *Sunday* on November 26 also proved to be a success, and the troupe was booked for a one-night stand on December 6 to present *Miss Temple's Telegram*. Prospective attendees may have wondered where that performance was to take place. Small newspaper notices identified the Miners' Union Theatre as the venue, while larger advertisements placed it at the Fernie Opera House, a designation ambitious managers of the new building apparently hoped to wrest from the long-established entertainment venue of the same name located nearby.[64] At the same time, the Russell troupe agreed to another two-night booking early in the New Year. When they arrived for that engagement, they found the venue had been renamed the Grand Theatre.[65] In contrast to their earlier performances, *Polly Primrose* on February 5 and *The Little Minister* on February 6 were announced with only minimal advertising in the *District Ledger* and the *Free Press*, and received no critical or subsequent comment in either newspaper.[66]

Occupied with bookings elsewhere, the Jeanne Russell troupe did not return to Fernie for two years. When it did—with a well-advertised week's engagement at the Grand Theatre in February 1912—critics were less generous than they had been previously. The reporter for the *District*

Ledger was not at all impressed with the performance on Monday evening of *The American Girl* or of Tuesday evening's *The Man from Home*. He was, however, enthusiastic about *Emanuella*, advertised on Thursday's bill by its alternate title, *Two Married Men*.

> One of the most remarkable portrayals which has been our lot to see, not only in this vast city of ours but in others, was that of Miss Jeanne Russell as "Emanuella" on Thursday last. The piece, which was written especially for Miss Russell, gave her ample opportunity to show her talent, and the consensus of opinion is that she got every ounce out of it. The second act of the piece alone was well worth the price of admission. A word of praise is also due to Ray F. Brandon...[67]

The *Free Press* agreed that the play was a "great success." Taken together, reviews from Fernie were comparable to those received elsewhere, generally applauding the performances of Jeanne Russell and Ray Brandon, but mentioning few other players and occasionally expressing some degree of criticism.[68] Still, expectations of a good attendance were high for both the Saturday matinee performance of *Charlie's Aunt* and the evening presentation of *The Half-Breed*. A special train was booked for eleven p.m. to allow theatre-going residents of Coal Creek to return home.

In addition to headliners Jeanne Russell and her husband Ray Brandon, sixteen members of the touring company had roles to play. One of them, a young British immigrant with no acting experience named William Pratt, had very recently joined the Russell troupe at Kamloops. Taking the stage name Boris Karloff, he played the role of Hoffman in *The Devil* in Nelson just before arriving in Fernie, and a Russian grand duke in *The Man from Home* in Calgary soon after leaving Fernie.[69] Both plays were presented during the week-long engagement at the Grand Theatre—*The Man from Home* on Tuesday, February 13, and *The Devil* on Friday, February 16. Only Russell and Brandon garnered individual mentions in the newspapers, but Karloff likely appeared in both performances. He was, after all, not being paid to remain in the wings.

Details of his time with the Russell players are sparse, and his tenure with them was brief. Following what the *Free Press* described as a "very successful week's engagement," the troupe caught the Sunday train heading for another week-long booking in Lethbridge, little knowing it would never play Fernie again. After a series of dates in southern Alberta and Saskatchewan that, according to Karloff, were financially disappointing, the players arrived in Regina just in time to be caught in the devastating tornado of June 1912. The Jeanne Russell Company fell apart and Karloff was out of a job, briefly finding work as a baggage handler for the CPR before moving to the United States. There was little to suggest he was heading for a career of distinction—on or off the stage.

Postscript

Some of the theatre-goers of 1912 in Fernie may well have become devotees of the cinema by the early 1930s. However, it seems unlikely they would have recognized the name Boris Karloff when *Frankenstein* was shown in Fernie at the Orpheum Theatre in May 1932. With the Russell troupe, Karloff had played no leading roles. Jeanne Russell was always the headliner and she probably never imagined that one of the bit players treading the boards with her at the Grand Theatre in Fernie would one day so completely eclipse her in historical memory. Following the disaster of the tornado in Regina, the touring company was re-established—again with Russell in the lead role. She continued performing into the war years, primarily in the western United States, and died in Utah in 1920 at the age of forty-four. Boris Karloff, an iconic figure in the history of cinema twice commemorated on the Hollywood Walk of Fame, was eighty-one when he died in England in 1969.

SEDITION AT MICHEL

THE INTERNMENT OF HERMAN ELMER

A s a German-born coal miner, Herman Elmer was an exceptional member of local union 2334 of the United Mine Workers of America (UMWA) at Michel. In a community populated by British, Canadian, American, Italian, Austro-Hungarian and Russian immigrants, his national origin was remarkable because it was so rarely encountered in the years just before the Great War. He stood for president of District 18 of the UMWA in December 1912 and then for vice-president in July 1913, polling impressively at each attempt; he became secretary of the Michel local union in August 1913 and worked successfully for a dramatic change to the constitution of District 18. Yet in the autumn of 1914, Elmer was arrested for sedition and imprisoned without trial. In both his arrest and his imprisonment, he was also exceptional. Throughout the remarkably turbulent war years to follow, the treatment of Herman Elmer would remain unique.

Elmer was born in the small seaside village of Kessin in northern Germany, *circa* 1877. It is not known how or precisely when he found his way to Michel, but surviving employment records indicate Elmer was first hired by the Crow's Nest Pass Coal Company in 1912. His name first appears in the *District Ledger*—the newspaper published by District 18—in January of that year, noting he was soon to participate in a debate on the topic of "Socialism versus Industrialism."[70] Elmer quickly became active in union politics and was elected one of the Michel local union's delegates to the District 18 convention held in Lethbridge in February. At that convention, he was instrumental in convincing delegates to endorse the principle of industrial unionism, but District 18 officials subsequently confirmed they did "not think it appropriate or in the best interests of organized labour" to publish letters Elmer was submitting to the *District Ledger*.[71] Undeterred, Elmer challenged the District 18 leadership by running for the office of president. He was handily defeated, but won the majority of votes at Michel, Frank, Blairmore and Taber.[72]

Following a serious injury due to a rock fall, Elmer returned to work in May 1913.[73] He also returned to the world of union politics, running unsuccessfully for the office of vice-president in District 18 in July. However, again he demonstrated how popular he had become with his fellow workers in the Michel local union, from whom he received as many votes as did the other five candidates combined. When the secretary-treasurer of the Michel local union declared he was moving to Spokane, Elmer stepped forward to replace him. At the age of thirty-six, he was soon receiving applause for the new energy he brought to union affairs.[74]

He immediately let it be known where he stood on the most important political issue facing the miners of District 18 during the summer of 1913. The British Columbia Federation of Labour was polling affiliates on a forty-eight-hour strike to protest the recent use of militia to break the Vancouver Island coal strike.[75] On September 14, the Michel local union voted in favour of that proposal. In a lengthy and strongly worded letter to the *District Ledger*, Elmer urged other local unions to do the same. He insisted that failure to support the miners of Vancouver Island "would stamp us as cowards who don't deserve a better fate than to remain slaves."[76] He was undoubtedly disappointed when the proposed protest strike did not find sufficient support across the province.

In January 1914, Elmer was again designated as a delegate to the annual District 18 convention scheduled to take place in mid-February. The Michel local union had submitted several resolutions and Elmer was charged with presenting the arguments for their adoption. One motion sought to justify strike action if a local union believed company violation of safety regulations endangered the safety of miners; another was a proposal to have the District 18 constitution align with socialist theory and objectives. Both resolutions were adopted by large majorities in amended form, though discussion was reportedly "heated at times."[77] The amendments would soon cause considerable controversy both at Michel and across the district. So too would the decision made at the convention to replace the union's first-past-the-post method of election with a preferential ballot.

As secretary—typically the most influential position in a local union—Elmer likely played a significant role in framing the resolutions

Michel submitted to the convention. That may explain the remarkably sharp criticism he soon directed against John Newman, a fellow miner who was the regular Michel correspondent for the *District
Ledger*. In his "Michel Notes" appearing in the *Ledger* soon after the
convention, Newman remarked that strike action seemed an excessive
response to safety violations.[78] Elmer's angry response, published in
the newspaper a week later, dismissed the criticism and noted that
the motion passed at the convention had been submitted by the local
union to which Newman belonged. He also clearly echoed the wording of the constitutional change:

> Let us always bear in mind that the working class and the
> employing class have nothing in common, and that the inter-
> est of the one class is diametrically opposed to the interest of
> the other. To produce for a class of parasites is bad enough
> under any circumstances, but to keep on creating wealth for
> them in the face of actual danger to the life and limbs of the
> producer would clearly demonstrate that the workers are
> only fit to be slaves.[79]

The argument was consistent with his support of the new political stance adopted at the District 18 convention, but Newman quickly
responded through the *Ledger* in a harshly worded riposte of his own.
Noting Elmer's "ridiculous and exaggerating remarks," Newman insisted the motion passed at the convention went beyond that initially
proposed by the Michel local union. He urged his fellow miners to
understand existing safety regulations "instead of switching to politics" and concluded "the brand of socialism that our local secretary
is trying his utmost to make predominant is as far in the distance as
Jupiter is from Mars..." Again Elmer responded, and, with a comment that drew a rebuke from the editor of the *Ledger*, alleged his
adversary seemed "better acquainted with a prayer book than with
the trend of the labour movement."[80] The drawn-out exchange indicates both men possessed some sharp edges. It also sheds light upon
the ongoing debates then common throughout District 18 amongst
adherents of competing strands of socialist thought and between socialists and non-socialists.

Elections for delegates to the Trades and Labor Congress and to
the Rocky Mountain Convention—a gathering of UMWA locals from
the western United States, Vancouver Island and District 18—were

held in April amidst much confusion over the preferential ballot. Elmer submitted an article to the *Ledger* attempting to explain the new
system to union members while admitting he did not yet fully understand it himself.[81] When the results of the vote from the local union at
Passburg in Alberta were announced, a correspondent to the *Ledger*
wrote that, despite knowing the numbers, miners there still didn't
know whom they had elected.[82] Results were so problematic the district declared them void, and, with no time for another vote, appointed the two leading vote-getters as delegates to the Rocky Mountain
Convention. Herman Elmer was one; the well-respected and long
serving District 18 executive member David Rees of Fernie was the
other. Upon their return in late May, Elmer and Rees jointly reported
that so little was accomplished the district had wasted its money in
sending delegates.[83]

But elections and conventions were entirely overshadowed in the
spring and summer of 1914 by terrible news from home and away.
Coal miners in Colorado—organized by the UMWA—had been engaged in a bitter strike for several months by the spring of 1914 and
were facing company-sponsored strikebreakers, state support for
mine owners and armed national guardsmen. In late April, those
guardsmen—who would commonly be called militia in Canada—at-
tacked a camp of strikers, killing at least nineteen men, women and
children. The outrage amongst mining communities in the Crowsnest was reflected in the continuing coverage by the *District Ledger*.[84]
Memories of the use of militia during the Vancouver Island coal strike
a year earlier were rekindled. The coincidental announcement that a
new militia unit—the 107th East Kootenay regiment—was soon to
be created and probably headquartered at Fernie was greeted with
considerable concern by miners in the region.

In mid-June, the focus of miners in District 18 shifted dramatically away from Colorado. On the morning of June 19, a massive
explosion at the Hillcrest mine in the Alberta Crowsnest killed 189
men. In a region painfully familiar with death in mining occupations,
the Hillcrest disaster set a grim new benchmark. It remains the worst
mining disaster in Canadian history, but for mining households
throughout the region in June 1914, more immediately it meant the
loss of life of friends and family and a reminder of the dangers each of
them faced on a daily basis. Collieries throughout the Crowsnest and
Elk Valley—acknowledged as the most dangerous mining operations

in Canada—suspended all work to express grief and solidarity.[85]

At the end of June, amidst the gloom and the fundraising effort for injured survivors and dependents of those killed at Hillcrest, the annual elections for district and local positions were taking place. Herman Elmer faced two challengers for the position of secretary of the Michel local union, one of whom was *Ledger* correspondent John Newman. Re-elected, Elmer took an active part in the debate over the renewed possibility of a general strike to support the locked-out miners on Vancouver Island. The British Columbia Federation of Labour was still divided on the question, and so too were the miners of District 18. At a four-hour meeting that attracted hundreds to the Socialist Hall in Fernie in late July, even those who favoured such a strike admitted the timing was not ideal. Elmer spoke at the meeting, insisting it was now or never, that there was "no time but the present for the worker."[86]

For the worker and everyone else, the outbreak of war in Europe a few days later changed everything. No one could even guess that more than four years of military conflict in Europe lay ahead, and few could appreciate how quickly and how dramatically the political landscape in the Crowsnest and throughout British Columbia would change. The *District Ledger* certainly did not, editorializing in early August: "So far as the Ledger is concerned, we have but one policy and that is the condemnation of war. The workers of the world have absolutely nothing to fight [each other] for, they have no quarrel."[87] In mid-August, it proclaimed that war was the result of the "deeply rooted disease" known as patriotism and suggested anyone suffering from an attack of patriotic feeling should ask himself, "Why should I be called upon to sing 'God Save the King' and then be asked to go and smash his uncle?"[88] Even as it became evident during the following weeks that patriotic fervour was sweeping aside previously held political beliefs, the newspaper—reflecting District 18 policy—continued its advocacy of internationalist principles.

Throughout August and September, patriotism was on display everywhere. Storefronts in Fernie and Michel were decorated with the Union Jack, fundraising efforts by the Red Cross and the Imperial Order Daughters of the Empire were launched with great success, and men rushed to volunteer. More than a hundred men—most of them miners— left the Elk Valley headed for training at Valcartier by the end of August. The *District Ledger* noted that patriotic suggestions were "thick as bees at swarming time."[89]

Michel, *circa* 1914. Fernie & District Historical Society 4882do

Just as prevalent were suspicions of people born in Germany and Austria-Hungary—residents of the Elk Valley and Crowsnest Pass who suddenly found themselves designated as enemy aliens. The first governmental attempt to address the concerns of the general public and enemy aliens alike was the proclamation of August 15. It guaranteed that German and Austro-Hungarian nationals would be accorded the protection of the law "so long as they quietly pursue their ordinary avocations." This guarantee was repeated in early September with the promise that non-British subjects "so long as they respect the law are entitled to its protection." However, passed through Parliament in August, the *War Measures Act* made clear the corollary of those guarantees: anyone deemed a threat to national security could be imprisoned without trial.[90]

The regular union meeting in Michel on Sunday, September 20, was unusually well attended. The draw was the attendance of the new president of District 18, William Phillips, who reportedly gave a "very able" address. Discussed thoroughly was the new requirement—just announced by the provincial government—that Austro-Hungarian and German nationals were to report to the provincial police on a weekly basis for the duration of the war. Phillips spoke of the union's anti-militarist policy and paid tribute to the German and Austro-Hungarian members of the local unions, just as he had been doing at meetings of local unions throughout District 18.[91]

By the first of two coincidences that would profoundly impact Herman Elmer, an order was issued in mid-September to organize the new regional militia regiment immediately. Recruitment began at the Fernie skating rink on the evening of September 18; on September 21, Company E of the 107th East Kootenay regiment also organized at Michel. Thirty-five men enrolled at Michel, most of them miners. On the afternoon of Sunday, September 27, the new recruits paraded from Michel Prairie to neighbouring Natal, accompanied by the Michel Band.[92] During the regular meeting of local union 2334 that same afternoon—perhaps with the music of the band distinctly audible—Elmer rose to answer a question from the floor about militia membership. He explained that the British Columbia Federation of Labour was considering asking affiliated organizations to debar any member who joined a militia unit. He also reiterated his personal opposition to the war as an internationalist socialist—a stance with which Michel union members were certainly familiar and which District 18 endorsed. Elmer confirmed that, in the European conflict, he was "a supporter of no particular country."[93] Rumours were soon circulating in Michel that German-born Herman Elmer had disparaged the militia and was hopeful of a German victory.

By the second fateful coincidence, on the day following the union meeting at Michel, militia officer Major William Ridgway Wilson of Victoria arrived in Fernie. Major Wilson was the officer-in-charge of the Department of Alien Reservists, freshly created by Military District 11. In that capacity, he was responsible for monitoring German and Austro-Hungarian males resident in British Columbia who were reservists in the armies of their home countries (as most European men of military age were). He had also made the arrangements necessary to establish two internment camps—one at Nanaimo and the other at Vernon—for those enemy aliens deemed to threaten national security. Wilson was in Fernie to instruct George Welsby, chief constable of the Southeast Kootenay Provincial Police, on the new provincial regulations requiring male German and Austro-Hungarian nationals to report to police stations.

Sanctioned by acting premier William Bowser in his capacity as attorney general, that plan very likely originated with Wilson as head of the Department of Alien Reservists. A month later, when the Dominion government introduced a national system of registration, Wilson soon complained it reduced his ability to register and monitor enemy aliens. He would later insist that Canadians with Germanic names should not be employed in internment camps.[94] There can be little doubt that Major Ridgway Wilson was as zealous in the exercise of his authority as was Herman Elmer in advocating industrial unionism and international socialism.

Elmer was convinced that employers were his clearly identified class enemy, but the injury he was about to sustain was not delivered by agents of industrial capitalism. Aware of Major Wilson's presence, two members of Michel local union travelled to Fernie on Monday, September 28, to advise him of the statements made by Elmer the day previous. So advised, Wilson did not hesitate. He concluded that Elmer was inciting discontent against the government and directed Chief Constable Welsby to arrest him for sedition. Acting under those orders, Welsby travelled to Michel and arrested Elmer on Tuesday, September 29. Initially unaware of the reason for his detention, Elmer was taken to the provincial jail in the basement of the courthouse in Fernie. Although he had done no more than confirm and endorse the anti-militarist policy of his union, his arrest on a charge of sedition could not be challenged. Having been arrested, no trial or legal process was required for a German national charged with sedition. Major Wilson's wartime authority and discretionary power were absolute.[95]

The *Fernie Free Press* of October 2 reported Elmer had been "taken into custody by the Provincial police acting under military instructions [for] preaching sedition and insulting the militia." Taking an undisguised swipe at the anti-militarist policy of the miners' union, the *Free Press* added that any other union members guilty of the same should share Elmer's fate.[96] In contrast, the *District Ledger* initially made no mention of the arrest, an omission that suggests the union—fearful that a printed defence of Elmer might also constitute sedition—was uncertain how to respond. President Phillips and board member David Rees addressed the issue in the privacy of the weekly meeting of the Michel local union on October 4.[97]

A week later, citing recent events on Vancouver Island and in Colorado, the *Ledger* sharply reminded the *Free Press* why the militia was not so highly regarded in mining communities. It also reported that Elmer was being treated well—as requested by union officials: "[He] is supplied with excellent food, both physical and mental, and at present [is] also taking the air under surveillance, which his many friends hope may in the near future be modified to release on parole."

The newspaper respectfully noted that this treatment had been courteously "granted by those who have charge of military affairs."[98]

The hopes of those many friends were not realized. On Saturday, October 10, Elmer left Fernie under police escort destined for the internment camp at Vernon, which had officially opened just three weeks earlier. He was registered on October 13 as prisoner number 14—one of the camp's first internees—undoubtedly optimistic he might soon be released and never imagining he was experiencing just the first of what would be five consecutive Octobers spent as a prisoner.[99]

As few facts are available, the motives of those responsible for Elmer's imprisonment invite speculation. The informants and those who spread the rumours through Michel after the fateful meeting of the local union may

David Rees pressed for the release of Herman Elmer. Fernie & District Historical Society DL-PF-1909-0270

have been motivated by personal animosity, by a desire to seek advantage in the internal politics of the union, or by a narrowly defined patriotism. It is highly unlikely they intended the consequence that befell Elmer. David Rees would later note they "sincerely regretted their action" once they saw its consequence.[100] For his part, if Major Wilson was aware of the policies of UMWA District 18, the knowledge caused him no hesitation; indeed, it may have been his intention to set an example in a region and in a union that seemed to be a stronghold of anti-militarist feeling. Possibly he wanted to warn enemy aliens to follow the new requirements of behaviour and registration, or he may simply have sought an internee for a camp that remained largely empty. In Herman Elmer, a German-born socialist who had not become a naturalized British subject and who had declined a clear opportunity to salute the Union Jack—even if only in a supposedly closed union meeting—he found his ideal candidate.

Elmer must have remained hopeful of release for some time,

aware that representations were being made to military authorities on his behalf. In conjunction with the British Columbia Federation of Labour, District 18 officials contacted the Department of Militia and Defence in January 1915, but were told the department saw "no reason to advise the release of Elmer."[101] District 18 renewed its efforts at its annual convention in Lethbridge in February. After a lengthy discussion, David Rees slammed "the insidious and unmanly action of the party who laid the information against Elmer" and introduced a strongly worded motion describing Elmer as a man whose actions were known at all times to be "above suspicion." Ending with a call for Elmer's release, the motion passed unanimously. The familiar political divisions within the union were nowhere to be seen.[102] But this second appeal — delivered through the offices of the Canadian Trades and Labor Congress — was no more successful than the first.[103] Elmer was then in his sixth month of internment.

Months turned into years. During his five years at Vernon, surviving documents refer to him only rarely and incidentally. There is nothing to suggest he was a troublesome internee. When the ceasefire in Europe was declared in November 1918, a third and final attempt — again by the Canadian Trades and Labor Congress and again headed by David Rees — was made. But circumstance and coincidence once more worked against Elmer. Major General William Otter, director of internment operations, had recently asked Major Nash, officer commanding at the Vernon internment camp, to provide names of those internees he considered to be troublesome or undesirable.[104] Nash replied that most of the prisoners at Vernon were "undesirable, troublesome or unwanted," and named those he believed held revolutionary views. In rejecting the appeal submitted by Rees, Otter had Nash's report freshly before him when he wrote: "[T]his man was interned for sedition, is of the class termed 'I.W.W.' and has since his arrest been more or less of a troublesome character."[105]

The Industrial Workers of the World (IWW) had been declared an illegal organization just two months earlier by Order-in-Council PC 2384. IWW was a label then broadly used by military and government officials to identify individuals favouring any form of labour activism. Being designated as such does not necessarily mean Elmer still favoured the principles of the IWW, but it does strongly suggest that he had not renounced his commitment to international socialism during his years in Vernon. With the focus of the government having shifted by 1919 to combatting foreign radicals and revolutionary socialism, the label IWW condemned him to continued detention.[106]

Denied due process of law as an enemy alien at the beginning of the war, Elmer—as an interned radical of foreign birth—was denied even a deportation hearing at war's end. By 1919 perhaps the longest-serving prisoner at Vernon, Herman Elmer was identified by Internment Operations as a "highly undesirable" internee when British authorities agreed to accept from Canada those individuals so designated. Accordingly, Elmer was deported aboard the *Empress of Britain*, which left Saint John, New Brunswick, for Liverpool on March 4, 1919. Elmer and the other ninety-nine deportees on the ship—all destined for re-internment at Alexandra Palace in North London— were the first internees deported from Canada.[107] Elmer was one of the signatories to a letter thanking the Swiss consul for his assistance during the deportation process. He spent a few days at Alexandra Palace, and, on March 19, 1919, was returned to Germany. The name Herman Elmer then disappears from the historical record as abruptly as it first appeared at Michel seven years earlier.

Postscript

The report in the *Fernie Free Press* a few days after his arrest in 1914 stated that Herman Elmer would be held at Vernon until the end of the war and then deported. Despite concerted efforts to secure his release, that is exactly what happened. Ironically, just as Elmer was leaving Saint John in 1919, people in Fernie were taking part in the bitter debate then raging nationwide over demands by returned soldiers to deport all enemy aliens. The debate was firmly grounded in post-war political and economic conditions, and was given extensive coverage by the *Free Press*. According to those newspaper reports, no one apparently chose to connect the issue to the arrest and imprisonment of Herman Elmer.[108]

The internment camp at Vernon closed officially on February 20, 1920, having been in operation for more than five years. It was the first to open in British Columbia and the last to close. During those five years, the Vernon camp housed approximately a thousand men, women and children from Germany and the ethnically diverse regions of what was then the Austro-Hungarian Empire. For most of the prisoners, their only apparent crime was their national origin. Each of them deserves to be remembered. One of them was Herman Elmer.

Doris and Dahlia

The Fast-Travelling Brunettes of Fernie

If it is true that every journey begins with one small step, I know when I took that step into Fernie history. My copies of *Progressive Fernie* and *Backtracking with the Fernie and District Historical Society* were neglected on my bookshelf for many years. Following a trip through Fernie with my daughter in 1990—my first visit to East Kootenay in twenty years—I gave them another look and began to wonder what more might lay hidden beneath the dust of decades. I soon visited Fernie again and stopped by the museum, then housed (but under eviction notice) in a cramped former church annex. In a corner of the small display case was a photograph that could not help but shock my post–Second World War eye: a swastika on the sweaters of smiling female hockey players. With explanations generously offered by museum volunteers Ella Verkerk and Bev Gregr, I learned something about the photograph, but wanted to know more. That women's hockey team invited me to enter the rich local history of the Elk Valley. It was an invitation I accepted without any understanding of the journey I was beginning, and I must admit the story of the Fernie Swastikas fascinates me still.

The photograph also revealed my own ignorance of Canadian history: I didn't know women played hockey a hundred years ago. I have since made two attempts to examine the history of the Fernie Swastikas. In *The Forgotten Side of the Border*, their story is presented with a local focus; in *Women on Ice*, that story is placed within the broader context of early women's ice hockey in British Columbia and Alberta.[109] While working on *Fernie at War*, I learned that women's hockey locally began a year earlier than I had once believed. The first reported game of women's ice hockey in Fernie actually took place in January 1918.[110] Each time, the impression lingered that a story remained unfinished.

Most notably in Rossland, women had long been playing ice hockey. In Fernie, an apparently unsuccessful attempt to form a women's team had taken place a decade earlier,[111] but the game played in 1918 was indeed an innovation. Apart from news items about organizations like the Imperial Order Daughters of the Empire and female auxiliaries of fraternal societies, it was also the first time women skated onto the pages of local newspapers and into the profoundly male-dominated history of Fernie. A century on and nationwide, the significance of female teachers, store clerks, bank employees and office stenographers then engaging in competitive sport is finally being recognized.

A 1923-24 postcard of the Fernie women's hockey team "The Swastikas."
Fernie & District Historical Society 1067

Interestingly, that first reported foray onto the ice in Fernie was framed as a charitable venture. Raising money for the war effort of the Red Cross was certainly an example of acceptable and established female endeavour. No such pretext was needed in 1919. In weekly Friday night contests throughout January and February, Biggs' Battlers, led by Trites-Wood sales clerk Edith Biggs, took on Dragon's Dreaders, captained by Bank of Commerce stenographer Mary Dragon. A roster was established in anticipation of playing external opponents, but lack of funds and preparation forced cancellation of all such plans.[112] Nevertheless, an end-of-season meeting at the home of player Doris Henderson made clear that a women's hockey club had been created.[113] In 1920 and 1921, the club did manage to take on opponents from out of town. The Fernie team performed creditably, but lost each of four contests to the powerful Calgary Regents.[114]

Following a meeting in early November 1921, players declared the team would henceforth be called the Fernie Red Wings. Just one week later, that decision was overturned when they formed a Swastika club. Swastika sports and social clubs were becoming popular, particularly amongst women and girls associated with Methodist and Presbyterian churches. If it can be said talismans do indeed bestow favour, the Fernie players had chosen theirs well. In 1922 and 1923, the Swastikas would prove to be at the top of their game. For the 1922 season, the Fernie women took to the ice with their new name, a distinct sense of confidence and a new look. Their modern hockey outfits were comprised of white knickers and red sweaters, each with the emblem of good fortune they had chosen—a large white swastika—sewn on the front.[115]

The emergence of the Swastikas in full hockey regalia in January 1922 would necessarily have come at considerable expense. Apart from teacher Florence Hamill, the players were all shop assistants, stenographers or bank employees. They worked hard at fundraising, but travel was expensive and the usual share of gate receipts typically was barely sufficient to cover obligations to visiting teams. Might the team have had an anonymous benefactor? Crow's Nest Pass Coal Company manager William Ritson Wilson had been admired for his generous support of community endeavours even before the famous Premier Mine made him a wealthy man. To mention just one example, he made the largest donation to the local baseball club's fundraising effort in 1922. However, he often preferred not to publicize his generosity.[116] His son, Bishop Wilson, a star player on the Fernie men's hockey team, would soon marry bank clerk Ella Fenwick, then in her second season with the women's team. Admittedly without supporting evidence, it is not unreasonable to wonder if the acquisition of those sparkling new hockey outfits might have been made possible because of financial support from William Ritson Wilson.

In 1922, the Swastikas played five games against powerful Calgary opponents, winning four, and allowing only two goals in the process. Their home game against the Regents drew a crowd of one thousand people. The *Calgary Herald* in 1922 described the Swastikas as a "world-beating team."[117] A year later, the same newspaper said they had become even better. The team eagerly accepted an invitation to the 1923 Banff Winter Carnival, where the winner of the annual women's hockey tournament would be declared the champion

FERNIE SWASTIKAS
1922

Dahlia Schagel, fourth from the left; Doris Henderson, fourth from the right.
Fernie & District Historical Society 6738

of western Canada. They won that title. Having easily dispatched the reigning champion Vancouver Amazons, the mantle was theirs unless another team could defeat them. Three times the aggressive Regents tried, but could not score a single goal.

And that statistic suggests the explanation for the success of the Fernie Swastikas: the defensive pairing of Dahlia Schagel and Doris Henderson. Each had been on the teams of earlier years—first identified by name in 1919—but had typically played forward positions. Schagel was described by the *Calgary Herald* in 1922 as a "fast travelling brunette," and the *District Ledger* once opined that Henderson skated too fast for a women's team.[118] The evident ability to defend their goalkeeper and then quickly turn the play toward the other end of the rink provided an advantage the Swastikas exploited fully in 1922 and 1923. Of course, speed and solid defence cannot win hockey games without effective offence. Each member of the team played her role well—Edith Biggs, for example, had a knack for scoring—but it was the combination of Schagel and Henderson that made the difference.[119]

The reception the champions received upon their return from Banff remains unique in the annals of women's ice hockey. Of course, it didn't hurt to have a proud father as the community's civic leader. When the morning CPR train arrived at the station, schools released the students and businesses closed up shop. The Fernie Pipe Band and the Royal North-West Mounted Police were ready to lead a procession of sleighs and cars from the station to the steps of city hall. From the lead sleigh, Mayor George Henderson waved the team mascot—about the size of a hand puppet, it was a golliwog dressed in Swastika colours—on the end of a miniature hockey stick.[120] Henderson, school board chairman Sherwood Herchmer and MLA Thomas Uphill made speeches of welcome and congratulations. On behalf of the players, team captain Schagel thanked the cheering crowd for the support that had made possible the Swastikas' participation in the Banff tournament.[121]

But somehow and suddenly the magic was gone. At the 1924 Banff Winter Carnival, following a solid victory over a strong opponent from Calgary, the Swastikas were stunned by losing to a first-year team from Canmore.[122] The championship was lost; there would be no cheering hometown crowd or triumphal parade. Perhaps symbols and talismans have only a limited amount of good fortune to bestow. In fact, team fortunes turned decidedly dark. Doris Henderson was suddenly stricken with an illness local doctors could not identify and died in late May. Distressed, Mary Dragon immediately resigned her position at the Bank of Commerce and returned to her home in Albion, New York.[123]

Another blow soon followed. New regulations adopted by the Alberta Amateur Hockey Association in 1925 effectively excluded the Swastikas—as a team based in British Columbia—from competition against their traditional opponents from Calgary. The Swastikas, without serious preparation and still suffering from the loss of Henderson and Dragon, declined an invitation to return to the Banff tournament.[124] Dahlia Schagel, expected at Banff as Carnival Queen, could attend only as a member of another team. In January, she was first reported to be captain of the Pincher Creek Felix Club, and then identified as a potential player for the Coleman Shamrocks, who were scheduled to make their first appearance at Banff. She did play for the Shamrocks at Banff (as did Edith Biggs, by then identified as Mrs. Kirkpatrick), and again received kudos for her play—but in a losing cause.

For one last time, the Swastikas regrouped. They took part in the tournament at Banff in 1926 and performed well, losing a close championship game to the Edmonton Monarchs, a team that included former Swastika Elaine Ross. The lack of pre-tournament play against competitive teams from Alberta and the loss of key players—Schagel, Henderson and Dragon—created a deficit that could not be overcome. Subsequently, apart from school-based games, women's hockey disappears from the annals of Fernie history.

Some stories lose their magic, their lustre, once they are told. This one does not. From a small, isolated, struggling, economically depressed community—far from the main currents of Canadian society and history—an unlikely sports team emerged to claim the highest title available in women's ice hockey. At the time, the winners of the annual Banff tournament were declared to be world champions. However, the choice of an emblem remains the team's misfortune. The symbol selected in November 1921 may have brought good fortune initially, but it was poisoned for all time in the decades that followed. One cannot help but wonder if the Fernie players might by now have claimed their rightful places in the British Columbia Sports Hall of Fame had they stuck with the decision to call themselves the Fernie Red Wings.

Postscript

Women's teams were established at Coleman in 1923 and at Cranbrook in 1925 specifically because of the example set by the Swastikas, but much more surprising is what happened in Fernie in 1958. For the first time in decades, a women's team was formed. Two convincing victories over the Old Crows of Blairmore are recorded.[125] What seems so shocking now is that the Fernie players of 1958 chose to call themselves the Swastikas. Clearly, it was an example of the triumph of local tradition/local legend over the changes wrought by the Second World War, when men and women from Fernie joined the Canadian Armed Forces to oppose the fascist threat. Of course, people in post-war Fernie recognized the stain the symbol had acquired. Yet when a team called the Swastikas took to the ice in 1958, no objection was recorded. Dahlia and Doris would have been pleased.

Tattered Dreams

The Working-Class Initiatives of 1909

In August 1909, barely a year after the great Fernie fire, an enthusiastic gathering of trades union members and their friends met to admire rooms yet under construction in the Miners' Union Building. Those assembled were members of the Fernie Workingmen's Club and Institute, and, though work on the interior rooms was far from complete, they liked what they saw. The Miners' Union Building was clearly going to be one of the most impressive architectural achievements of Fernie's ambitious reconstruction process, and the fledgling Workingmen's Club had found a home in it. In the optimism of the moment, no one in the club or the miners' union would have predicted the troubled future that lay ahead.

The Workingmen's Club and Institute had been formed several months earlier.[126] Clearly intending to follow the model of such clubs in the United Kingdom, those present at the founding meeting in January were well aware of the middle-class perception that social organizations of workingmen were little more than "drinking dens."[127] Speakers emphasized the educational benefits that could be offered—particularly to young men, who, without such a club, "had no place to go but to the saloons." For members who might want a drink, it was agreed beer should be provided at a reasonable price, but local lawyer Louis Eckstein noted the club would provide more than just refreshment, for there would also be a reading room and a games room for checkers, billiards, cards and dominoes. In attendance was Frank Sherman, president of District 18 of the United Mine Workers of America. He offered to provide good books to start the library and noted a gymnasium should be considered because of the need to develop in young men both mental and physical powers. The enthusiastic gathering set the membership fee at $5 and elected

F. Woodyard as president, Thomas Biggs as secretary and a twelve-man planning committee that included T.H. Wray and Thomas Uphill.[128]

The new organization was inspired not only by workingmen's clubs in the United Kingdom, but also by an example very much closer to home. The Coal Creek Literary and Athletic Association had operated successfully at Coal Creek since 1905. Its clubhouse included all the facilities mentioned at the founding meeting of Fernie's Workingmen's Club and Institute — a bar, library and reading room, games rooms, gymnasium, a meeting room — and also a public hall used for community events. The building had been constructed by the Crow's Nest Pass Coal Company at no cost to the association, which then operated the facility through monthly membership fees. Fundamentally, the vision of the Fernie Workingmen's Club and Institute was to follow the Coal Creek model in all respects.[129]

Although the newspaper report made no mention of where the club rooms were to be located, members knew very well that the Miners' Union Building would be their home. That building had been long anticipated. In May 1904, in the downtown core destroyed by fire a month earlier, Gladstone local union 2341 of the UMWA purchased a large lot adjacent to the Central Hotel on Victoria Avenue and announced its intention to construct a two-storey building to accommodate "a concert hall" on the lower floor and union offices above.[130] The lot remained vacant for four years, but in January 1908 the union declared it was ready to proceed. A month later, it became clear this would not be just the modest union hall first imagined in 1904. The projected cost of plans by architects Campbell and McLaren of Vancouver would be in excess of $30,000.[131] The building would provide union offices and meeting rooms on the upper floor, a theatre and two commercial storefronts on the ground floor, and substantial cellar capacity beneath. Construction was to begin immediately with an intended completion date of early November.[132]

Financial arrangements may have included a bank loan, but relied primarily on a payroll deduction approved by members of the local union. In this last respect, the example of Coal Creek again provided guidance. The furnishings and equipment for the Coal Creek Literary and Athletic Association clubhouse had been paid for through a temporary payroll deduction. For the Miners' Union Building in Fernie, the payroll deduction would go toward the costs of construction, while revenues from the theatre and storefronts and

Shares in the Building Fund of the Gladstone Local Union cost a dollar each. Fernie & District Historical Society 7043do

the rental of the hall and meeting room were expected to service any debt and cover operating costs. The Gladstone local union thus became an investor in commercial real estate.

Construction got underway, but was soon delayed as bricks were not readily available in the summer of 1908. More dramatically, when materials were finally all on site, the fire that roared down Victoria Avenue in August destroying everything in its path did not spare the partially completed Miners' Union Building. Uninsured losses for the union were initially reported to be between $15,000 and $25,000, though the lesser figure of $8,000 was later confirmed.[133] It was a setback of staggering proportion. Although the decision was quickly made to rebuild, the loss imposed an additional burden on the already stretched finances of the local union.

Acknowledgement of that burden came at the annual convention of District 18 in February 1909, when the local union asked for a loan of $5,000 to finish construction. That request was not approved by UMWA headquarters in Indianapolis. However, the Gladstone local union incorporated as a society, thereby gaining the legal status required to offer shares in a corporation. In April, District 18 agreed to accept shares in the building in lieu of dues the local union owed but could not pay because construction demands were consuming all its available financial resources. District 18 thereby became an investor in the venture, effectively acting as a mortgage lender.[134]

The pace of construction picked up. With work still ongoing, the Miners' Union Building was beginning to function. As secretary of the local union, David Rees also acted as manager of the building. He secured a rental agreement for one of the storefronts in March, made arrangements with fraternal societies and other unions to hold their meetings in the union hall, and acted as booking agent for the opera house. By early summer, the union hall and reading room upstairs were essentially finished, while work on the opera house, lower floor and cellar was being rushed. In mid-August, the Fernie Industrial and Provident Co-operative Society moved into the north-side storefront and plans for the cellar were modified to accommodate the Workingmen's Club and Institute.

The social centre for the club—complete with billiard table, pool table and bar—was to be located there, while the club's library, reading and meeting rooms would be on the upper floor. As the *District Ledger* reported, the inaugural gathering of the club in its new rooms took place in mid-August:

> The Fernie Workingmen's club was opened this week in their spacious rooms in the new Miners hall. Hundreds of trade unionists, and some not members of any union have affiliated with this club, and as they have received their license the results will be beneficial and gratifying to all.[135]

The editor of the *Ledger* was not always a reliable source for numbers, but there is no doubt membership was impressive. Three months earlier, Provincial Police Inspector John McMullin was advised eighty men had already paid their $5 registration fees.[136]

When the club incorporated as a society, its application listed all the educational and recreational purposes first identified at the organizational meeting, added an intention to build a bowling green for use by members, and pledged to work "for the suppression and minimizing by all legitimate means of intemperance among workingmen." That theme was emphasized by club lawyer Louis Eckstein who advised the superintendent of provincial police that: "One of the [club's] principal features is that it will not allow the sale of anything but beer, it being the opinion of the workingmen that by selling beer alone, the evil of drinking will be minimized."[137]

Both the union hall and the opera house were soon in operation. In late September, with permanent seating not yet installed and electricity not yet connected, the opera house was the venue for a speech by American socialist Bill Haywood, while the union hall was booked for a smoker by the Fraternal Order of Eagles. In October, the funeral of former District 18 president Frank Sherman took place at the union hall, and the Fernie Philharmonic Society hosted the first performance held at the opera house. With a provincial election underway, the Socialist candidate launched his campaign at the union hall, and local Liberals booked a date at the opera house for November. When lighting and permanent seating were finally in place, itinerant theatre companies were booked for dates in November. The Miners' Union Building was open for business.

The entire community was impressed. On the upper floor were located the union office and meeting hall, the library and the reading room. The opera house and dressing rooms occupied the whole of the main floor behind the two rented storefronts—the north side housing the Fernie Industrial and Provident Co-operative Society store; the south side occupied by the Heintzman and Company piano showroom. In the basement were the boiler and engine room, storage space for the Co-operative Society store and the still unfinished rooms of the Workingmen's Club and Institute. The games room was ready, and a large billiard room was being fitted up. The Elk Valley Brewing Company had installed its impressive taps at the bar where drinks were to be "sold to members and friends at as near cost as possible." Six lavatories

WORKINGMEN'S
CLUB and INSTITUTE ....

RULES and REGULATIONS
Located at Fernie, B. C.

On the cover page of this draft copy, a hopeful acorn represents the club's aspirations. Royal BC Museum and Archives GR 97, vol. 2, File L-Z "of the most approved and sanitary design" were located at various points throughout the building, and the words "Gladstone Local" inscribed in tile at the front entrance reflected the proprietary sense of achievement evidently felt by members of the local union.[138]

Touring theatre groups attracted large audiences. By the end of the year, a professional manager was hired to operate the opera house, which was being touted as the finest such west of Winnipeg and was soon renamed the Grand Theatre to reflect that status. The Workingmen's Club began games tournaments for its members, and, although a water pipe burst during the Liberals' election meeting, all indications were that the future held nothing but promise for the Gladstone local union's commercial venture. So positive did it all seem that the miners' local union at Michel planned to poll members at the end of December on its proposal to build a union hall and store.[139]

POLITICS, BEER AND FINANCES

Without warning, the prevailing sense of optimism received a sharp and sudden check. During Christmas week, the Department of the Attorney General notified the chief constable of provincial police at Fernie that the application from the Workingmen's Club for renewal of its liquor licence was being refused. Stating only that a renewal "would not be in the public interest," the decision was greeted with dismay and anger. On behalf of the club, lawyer Louis Eckstein requested an explanation for the refusal, but received no reply. The editor of the *District Ledger* demanded a definition of "public interest" and argued that the hotel owners of Fernie—anticipating considerable loss of revenue at their saloons—had used their political influence with Conservative MLA William Ross to quash the licence of the Workingmen's Club.[140]

The hotel owners were indeed politically powerful and had used their influence once before to quash a nascent club in Fernie. In early 1906, the Elk Valley Club opened at rooms on Victoria Avenue as a less exclusive version of the established social centre for business and professional men known as the Fernie Club. While not objecting to the existence of the Fernie Club (of which some were members), the hoteliers called upon city authorities "to suppress" the Elk Valley Club, arguing hotels should be protected against competition from a club possessing no liquor licence, which hotels were required to purchase annually. Accordingly, in June, city police raided the Elk Valley Club, and its manager was found guilty in police court of the bylaw infraction. The club was shuttered and the fines levied were so substantial the manager languished for a time in the city jail unable to pay them.[141]

The provincial refusal to renew the licence of the Workingmen's Club was a clear blow to the social vision of its founders, and the club would certainly have a reduced appeal to potential members. It was also a blow to club finances. Fewer members and no bar receipts signalled a significant loss of potential revenue. At the annual convention of District 18 in Lethbridge in February, it was apparent how badly revenue was also needed by the building's owners. Despite having its debt cleared by the share purchase in April 1909, the Gladstone local union was again six months in arrears with dues owed by the end of the calendar year. The debt to District 18 had grown to nearly $6,800 as local union funds were still being directed to the financial requirements of the new building. The guest speaker at the convention, a past president of the Western Federation of Miners, urged that no local union be allowed to erect a hall with district approval, arguing that the Gladstone local, "burdened with debt on account of erecting a hall, should be an object lesson." The convention paid attention: it approved a request from the Michel local to build a union hall, but only after "the indebtedness of the Fernie local had been paid up to the district."[142]

At the same time, during a session of the legislature in Victoria, Bowser belatedly offered an explanation of why the Workingmen's Club licence was not renewed. Taking personal responsibility for the decision, he said "a real club" would provide games and billiards rooms, a reading room and lounge. He claimed it was necessary to leave the building to move from one room to another and that the club was "composed in the most part of a bar and a supply of beer." Bowser was echoing the report he received from Provincial Police Inspector John McMullin, who had toured the yet unfurnished rooms in early December and noted he could not help "being impressed with the fact that the bar was the salient feature, at any rate at the present time."[143]

Fernie's newspaper editors reacted with predictably opposite assessments of the cancellation of the licence. The inspector's report contained no recommendation regarding the liquor licence. However,

Wallace at the *Free Press* wrote McMullin found "the club was run almost entirely for the booze end of the business and reported that in the best interests of the citizens of Fernie the license should be cancelled." In contrast, the editor of the *District Ledger* was scathing in response to Bowser's statement, pointing out that the facilities at the club included all the rooms Bowser said it lacked and more. He urged the attorney general to restore the licence, insisting that the features of the ideal "real club" Bowser had identified provided a perfect description of the Workingmen's Club in Fernie.[144]

Enthusiasm for the club clearly suffered from the lack of a liquor licence. In the summer of 1910, membership was offered for just $1.[145] At year-end, anger and accusation revived when the licence application was refused a second time. Club secretary T.H. Wray demanded an explanation. In response, Bowser referred to another unfavourable report by a new inspector who found beer available even in the absence of a licence, and to the use of club rooms as headquarters for the Socialist Party candidate in a recent by-election. He made no mention

Concerned union officials look down as the fire wagon responds to an alarm at the Central Hotel in July 1910. The south-side storefront remains unoccupied. Fernie & District Historical Society FFP 0590

of reasons offered for the initial refusal, nor of the new inspector's observation that "There is not the need of a club [in Fernie] that there is at Coal Creek, as there are hotels there." Club officials noted the beer taps were still in place in hopes of a renewed licence, and agreed the Socialist Party did indeed hold its meetings in the new union building, just as it had in the old. The impression remained that any excuse to withhold a licence would do and that political influence from Fernie's hotel owners had determined the matter.[146]

But the union managers of the Miners' Union Building had other concerns. The Heintzman piano showroom quickly proved unsuccessful and closed. Intending to compete with the Fernie Opera House, the installation of a "moving picture machine" at the Grand brought a second cinema to Fernie in March 1910, but a third competitor in the entertainment field, the Isis Theatre, also began showing films in 1911. Some fraternal societies preferred to hold their meetings at the Knights of Pythias hall. Although the Grand was leased for $225 a month, revenue from all sources was simply not meeting expectations.[147] Repairs and renovations—a burst pipe and small cellar fire in 1909; a new roof in 1910; improvements to deficient seating in the gallery and redecorating the foyer at the Grand in 1911—added considerably to regular maintenance costs. A proposal to borrow $25,000 from District 18 in exchange for a mortgage on the building in August 1911 was rejected and the local union fell further behind in dues owed to the district. It was necessary to impose a levy of $1 per month on all members to cover operating expenses of the building.[148]

FACING CHANGED REALITIES

It was clear to all that a liquor licence for the Workingmen's Club would not be granted and that the dream of a traditional working-class social club was over. In September 1912, the local union agreed to take over the club and made the reading and recreation rooms available to all members at no charge.[149] Although the name was unchanged, the Workingmen's Club had been succeeded by a miners' club. However, the buoyant local economy of 1909–1911 had suffered a sharp reversal, adding further strain to the financial situation of the Miners' Union Building. This was particularly true in connection with the Grand Theatre. Competing with both the Grand and the Isis, the rival Fernie Opera House rebranded itself as the Orpheum in 1912 to focus more specifically on film presentations. By the end of 1913, "under new management" was being announced for the fifth time at the Grand in just four years. The consequences were felt individually by members of the Gladstone local union and collectively by District 18. The dollar-a-month levy was continued in 1912 and 1913, although it was acknowledged the money thus collected was not enough to cover operating expenses. At the same time, the local union fell even further behind in dues payments. By the end of 1913, indebtedness to the district had ballooned to $20,000.[150]

The Workingmen's Club made one final serious attempt to attract revenue and a broader clientele. The basement rooms were redecorated at the end of 1913 and it was no longer necessary to be a member of the club or the local union in order to enter. The billiard tables were refitted and, in a very progressive move, women were encouraged to "acquire skill with cue and ivory." The refreshment bar offered cigars, soft drinks and candies. The new manager organized billiards tournaments with prizes available, had tokens minted to be exchanged for merchandise at the refreshment bar, and advertised heavily in the *District Ledger*.[151]

But little seems to have changed. The advertisements for the Workingmen's Club stopped abruptly at the end of December. Yet another new manager took charge at the Grand in the New Year, and a new tenant— Branch 17 of the Socialist Party of Canada— occupied the south-side storefront for just a few months before moving into its own building in March 1914. Unhappy with the inadequate heat supplied during the winter, the Co-operative Society also relocated after five years' tenancy in the north-side storefront.[152] With no change in the indebtedness of the Gladstone local union, any patience

Token issued by the Workingmen's Club, probably *circa* 1912–1913. Images courtesy of Ronald Greene

still remaining amongst District 18 officials was wearing thin. After a lengthy and heated debate at the annual convention in Lethbridge in February 1915, delegates urged "that steps be taken to force the collection of individual loans made from the District Funds" and passed a motion directing the district executive to "enquire into the affairs of the Gladstone Local Union."[153]

Changes in management at the Grand were announced with dizzying frequency. A new manager in February 1914 introduced amateur nights, one of them featuring a boxing match on roller skates, comic songs by local miners and five reels of motion pictures—all for an admission of just 10 or 20 cents.[154] The booking of touring theatre groups stopped in the summer of 1914, but was resumed by December. Another shutdown followed in the new year until a new lessee—promising to present Pantages theatrical performances every week—undertook renovations and repairs to the seats and resumed bookings in May 1915.[155] The Pantages-only approach failed quickly. In the autumn of 1916, the focus shifted to motion pictures as the projection room was refitted and another hopeful lessee began presenting blockbuster films. D.W. Griffith's now notorious *Birth of a Nation* and Charlie Chaplin's *The Champion* were amongst the attractions drawing good audiences. With the return of prosperity throughout the region, Fernie became an entertainment hub as the Grand, the Isis and the Orpheum all offered quality film presentations to an eager public.

At the same time, Abraham Haddad—the clothing and dry-goods merchant—proved to be the stable tenant long sought for the south-side storefront. Yet such encouraging signs were always overwhelmed by less favourable developments. The successful venture into motion picture presentations ended when the lessee abruptly left his responsibilities in the hands of an assistant in April 1917. The Gladstone local union sued for damages, but was forced to resume direct control of the theatre once again.[156] Miner Francis Brindley was named as manager and the theatre stopped booking films, describing itself as an "opera house, travelling show house." The first show booked was a big revue advertising itself as "A Merry Musical Comedy Company Surrounded by Girls."[157]

The financial situation of the local union remained precarious. In the generally prosperous year of 1917, barely a dozen properties were seized by the city for unpaid taxes, but the Miners' Union Building was one of them. The union faced the prospect of losing title to its primary asset when it was acquired by "a syndicate of local capitalists" for $2,400 at the city tax sale in October.[158] The union then won its suit against the former manager and was able to retain ownership by paying the overdue taxes. Clearly, the financial burden deriving from the dream of 1909 was weighing heavily on the miners of Fernie and Coal Creek, and the opinion that the building had become "a white elephant" was gaining currency amongst them.

A Building Lost, a Dream Forgotten

The end of the Great War generated great optimism amongst working people that the world in general and their place in it would be improved significantly. In Fernie, expressions of that optimism echoed the hopes and aspirations of those who built the Miners' Union Building and founded the Workingmen's Club and Institute a decade earlier. In the early months of 1919, members of the Gladstone local union gave almost unanimous support to the vision of a better world proffered by the One Big Union (OBU) as they prepared to break from the United Mine Workers of America. Local union leader Harry Martin—a strong supporter of the OBU—took over management at the Grand. The reinvigorated Workingmen's Club decided to renovate the former Knights of Pythias hall and made plans to move.[159] In April, just a month before the beginning of the district-wide strike intended to achieve recognition of OBU, it was announced that another hopeful lessee had signed a two-year contract to manage the Grand and resume the booking of films.[160]

The new arrangement was short-lived. During the four months the strike lasted, a new Heintzman Concert Grand piano was installed and an advertising campaign conducted that was more extensive than any attempted previously. However, the remarkably large advertisements appearing each week in the pages of the *District Ledger* and the *Free Press* concealed the fact that, because of the strike, miners and practically everybody else in the region had little money to spend on leisure. As the strike effectively became a lockout and continued into August, both the Grand motion picture show and the *District Ledger* newspaper closed down.[161] The Gladstone local union imposed a new assessment of 25 cents per month to pay for taxes, water and electricity at the Miners' Union Building. It was not enough. At the end of September, for the second time in just three years, the building was again sold to a group of local investors for unpaid taxes, even as the OBU leadership of the local union refused to relinquish control of the miners' offices located within it.[162]

With the strike finally over and the UMWA's Francis Brindley back as manager, the Grand resumed booking community groups and theatrical touring companies in November. In March 1920, both performances of *Biff, Bing, Bang*—advertised as "an all-man girl show"—by the nationally famous Dumbells played to full houses, just the most notable of a long series of successful bookings as the Grand began a rare period of stability. However, to reclaim the union offices, the UMWA was forced to sue. Finally acknowledging their defeat, OBU officials did not contest the suit and were escorted from the building by the sheriff in May 1920.[163]

Back in control of the entire building, UMWA officials cannot have been pleased by what they found. The new Heintzman piano had been vandalized and financial obligations were accumulating. Taxes and fire insurance for 1919 remained unpaid, those for 1920 were due, the electricity bill was nearly two years in arrears, and $875 was owed to the Co-operative Society. The date upon which the title to the building would be lost permanently was rapidly approaching. William Hunter soon succeeded Brindley as building manager, but to redeem ownership and pay overdue accounts, the Gladstone local union—with virtually no funds at its disposal—faced a bill of nearly $5,000.[164] When tangled affairs were finally sorted, the local union was paying monthly rent for its offices and club rooms to the building's new owner: District 18. And district officials were not interested in operating an entertainment centre. The Dumbells' *Full o' Pep* in May 1923 marked the end of the Grand's participation in theatrical circuits.

At the same time, the local union announced it was moving its offices to the former *District Ledger* building. Still, the old dreams retained their allure. In June 1923, District 18 accepted an offer from the Gladstone local union to purchase the building for the sum of $4,100, with an initial payment of $1,000 and a promise to pay the balance with interest in January 1925. When the local union at the eleventh hour declared it was unable to meet that obligation, ownership of the building remained with District 18.[165] And while proprietary matters were slowly being resolved, the miners' Workingmen's Club made a successful attempt at resurrection that was initially successful. Reinventing itself as the Fernie Literary and Athletic Association in 1920, the club moved to new premises and thrived, finally providing members with the long-desired gymnasium and acquiring a liquor

licence in 1924. However, a remarkably severe fine of $1,000 for sell-
ing beer on a Sunday in 1926 undermined the club's financial position
and contributed to its demise at the end of the decade. By then, echoes of
the working-class dreams of 1909 were barely audible.[166]

A visual testament to those dreams did remain, but the Miners' Union Building—so proudly opened in 1909—became both an
anomaly and a slowly decaying monument to the aspirations it once
represented. After local miners abandoned the UMWA in 1924–1925,
the building received only basic repairs and minimal maintenance.
William Hunter, the last president of the UMWA-affiliated Gladstone
local union, continued to manage the building on behalf of the international union's headquarters in Indianapolis. Finally despairing
that local miners might renew their affiliation, the UMWA decided
its real estate in Fernie was not worth the effort and expense ownership entailed. When taxes were not paid in 1929, the old *District
Ledger* building became civic property. So too did the Miners' Union
Building. Offers to purchase were invited, but this time there were no
prospective buyers and no belated settling of accounts. The City of
Fernie—itself in deepening financial trouble as the Depression took
hold—reluctantly became the owner of record in October 1930.[167]

The city used the Grand Theatre for civic assemblies and rented
the facility whenever possible (typically for $10 each time), but the
building continued to receive only minimal maintenance. For many
years the theatre remained the community's largest meeting and performance hall. The UBC Players visited regularly, annual high school
concerts were well attended, political issues and election rallies often generated packed houses. The movie projection room was also
occasionally used to show educational films to children. During the
Second World War, bands touring to raise funds for Victory Loans
frequently performed at the Grand. The City of Fernie was delighted
finally to find a buyer in 1946 for what was by then being described
as a "partial ruin."[168]

Postscript

Thoroughly renovated as a modern cinema, the former Miners'
Union Building was revived as the Vogue Theatre in May 1947. For
the first time in many years, the Orpheum Theatre—sole survivor
of the entertainment venues operating during the latter days of the

Great War—had a competitor. Movie-goers again had a choice until the smaller Orpheum was acquired by the owner of the Vogue and shut down. The editor of the *Free Press* had greeted the end of cinematic presentations at the Grand in 1919 by insisting Fernie was not big enough to support more than one movie house.[169] The same apparently was true thirty years later.

The Vogue Theatre remains in operation today, proudly pointing to the building's historic role in providing entertainment for over a century. On the facade, only the date of construction—still embedded in the pediment—has survived renovations to suggest there could be far more to the history of this building than the casual observer might possibly imagine.

Empire of Suds

Albert Mutz and Brewing
in the Elk Valley

A s the number of craft breweries in British Columbia contin-
ues to grow apace, the history of ales and lagers of quality is
often presented as a tale of recent origin, with a few token
nods to the pioneers of the 1980s. However, brewing pioneers in this
province were well at work a hundred years earlier. As the twentieth
century began, British Columbia was home to three dozen independent brewers, each offering customers a range of local products and
each experimenting with recipes that could potentially expand that
range. One of the longest-surviving of those historic breweries was
located in the remote Elk Valley, a coal-mining region in the south-
eastern corner of the province.

The origins of brewing in that region are found nearly 100 kilometres to the west, at Fort Steele, where partners Fritz Sick and
Fredrick Kaiser opened for business in 1898. They expected to find a
ready market in territory served by the new Canadian Pacific branch
line running from Lethbridge in Alberta to Kootenay Lake in British
Columbia. However, the decision to route that line through Cranbrook—rather than through Fort Steele as anticipated—meant the
small brewery was in a relatively isolated location. By 1900, its owners were faced with the choice of closing or relocating. Fritz Sick and
two new partners—Albert Mutz and his brother-in-law, George Hil-
ton Scott—decided on relocation, but not to Cranbrook. They would
build in the Elk Valley—close to the Canadian Pacific branch line—
on a three-acre site with an ideal water source just west of the new
boomtown called Fernie.

Like Fritz Sick, Albert Mutz had immigrated initially to the
United States from the Freiburg area in Germany in the mid-1880s.
Both were employed at the Puget Sound Brewery in Tacoma in the

early 1890s,[170] but while Sick soon saw opportunity in Spokane, Mutz moved to Canada in 1894. He settled near Fort Steele, where he built and operated a small hotel and had some success as a prospector. He must have been surprised in 1898 to learn of his former colleague's plans to open a brewery locally.[171] Two years later, when Sick was in dire need of operating capital, Mutz and George Scott stepped forward to become co-owners of the Fort Steele brewery. The decision to relocate quickly followed.

Sick, Mutz and Scott transported moveable equipment from Fort Steele as construction got underway on Cokato Road, just south of Fernie. Advertisements began appearing in the *Fernie Free Press* in March 1901, offering beer and porter "sold by barrel, keg or bottled" by "Sick, Mutz & Co., Props." However, Fritz Sick—apparently uncomfortable within the partnership—was already considering other possibilities. Just as production was beginning in late April, he sold his interest to his partners for the sum of $10,000.[172] George Scott was designated as business manager, but left brewing matters in the hands of his brother-in-law. From the first days of its operation, therefore, what quickly became the popular designation of the business as "Mutz's brewery" was an accurate one.

Proudly posing on the steps of the new brewery for a commemorative photograph, Albert Mutz was also standing at the threshold of his long association with Fernie. He would soon join the Fernie Board of Trade as he began to establish his reputation as the "genial German who understands beer manufacture from top to bottom."[173] The Fort Steele Brewing Company had chosen its new location wisely. Sales in the Fernie region were strong and the impressive new brewery—with decorative crenellations atop its facade and the capacity to produce approximately 1,000 barrels a month—was able to meet all demands from the string of coal-mining communities located along the river valley and across the provincial border into the Crowsnest Pass.

It soon became clear that Mutz possessed both ambition and access to capital. In the summer of 1902, the company announced it would proceed at once to erect a large brewery at Frank. Promotional advertising at Christmas indicated the facility was in operation, but work on what Mutz called his "branch brewery" was still ongoing at the end of the year.[174] He also purchased a property at Blairmore with the intention of building a brewery there.[175] Typically, in British

Columbia, brewers invested in the hotel industry and Mutz was no exception. In 1903, he acquired a half interest in the Imperial Hotel in Frank and full ownership of the Coleman Hotel.

In January 1904, Mutz and Scott expressed confidence in their venture by incorporating and jointly becoming majority shareholders in the Fort Steele Brewing Co., Ltd. They then immediately acquired the East Kootenay Bottling Works operation in Fernie at a cost of $5,000.[176] The company was soon marketing a variety of soft drinks (then called "aerated waters")—products to attract the more temperance-minded consumer.

By 1899, Charles Williams had replaced Kaiser as co-owner of the brewery at Fort Steele. Facing the camera, Fritz Sick and his four children stand to the left of the dog. Fernie & District Historical Society FFP 1303

Albert Mutz and his children, George Scott, a dog and employees gathered for a photograph in 1901. The image was then used in advertising. Fernie & District Historical Society FFP-(02)-0095

While Mutz had quickly become a dominant figure in the local brewing industry and hotel business, he was not the only brewer interested in the region. The Crow's Nest Pass Brewing Company began production at Morrissey in July 1903.[177] The new brewery was expected to compete with the larger operation at Fernie, but soon found itself in difficulty with creditors. In less than a year, the Crow's Nest Pass Brewing Company was bankrupt. The building, equipment, stock and land were sold at public auction for $2,500 in May 1904. The purchaser was variously reported to be either Mutz personally or the Fort Steele Brewing Company. If plans to resume production at Morrissey were considered, they were permanently shelved when the brewery was destroyed by fire just two months later.[178]

Another competitor soon emerged, this time in Fernie itself. In 1903, brewer Nicholas Klausman arrived in Fernie and found local investors in hotel owners William Eschwig and Sarah Jennings. They launched their Fernie Brewing Company in late 1904. The venture showed every sign of being successful, but just six months later, Eschwig and Jennings both decided to offer their interests in the brewery to Klausman—an offer he would not or could not afford to take up.

Mutz, attempting what was clearly a hostile takeover, then approached the hotel owners with a generous proposal. It was soon understood that the partnership of Eschwig, Jennings and Klausman had been dissolved and that the Fort Steele Brewing Company had purchased the rival brewery. Mutz announced the facility would be closed until production demands on Cokato Road might require its capacity, while Klausman—much like Fritz Sick four years earlier—left Fernie to explore brewing possibilities elsewhere.[179]

Albert Mutz, *circa* 1905. Fernie & District Historical Society FFP-(05-06)-0073

Like the operation at Morrissey, the brewery never did resume production. The Fort Steele Brewing Company apparently was interested in a local monopoly and possessed the financial resources required to pursue that objective. The workers at Cokato Road immediately understood the implications of there being only one brewer in the region. Just a week after the purchase of the Fernie Brewing Company, they went on strike for a wage increase of 25 cents per day, a demand to which Mutz and Scott quickly agreed.[180]

Just as Sick had done at Fort Steele, Mutz and Scott at Fernie employed German immigrants in positions with the chief responsibilities—especially those of a brewmaster—and provided on-site accommodation for more than a dozen employees. The brewery output for the month of March 1905 increased to 1,200 barrels, each containing thirty-two gallons.[181] Mutz was also experimenting, making a bock beer available "for a few days only" in May. Prospects for the Fort Steele brewery were bright and the company paid its first dividend at the end of 1904.[182] Nevertheless, George Scott soon left Fernie and began to withdraw from the company, selling his shares to Mutz some months later. Both brewing and business matters were henceforth entirely in the hands of Albert Mutz. "Mutz's brewery" had indeed become Mutz's brewery.[183]

However, as Mutz well knew, competition for the local trade was inevitable. Geographically, that competition came from all directions. The Cranbrook Brewing and Malting Company opened in 1904, but quickly ran into financial difficulties. Again demonstrating his

Advertisement in *Fernie Free Press Souvenir Edition,* 1907. Fernie & District Historical Society FFP-(07)-0043

quest to maintain a regional monopoly, Mutz managed to purchase the defunct brewery in 1906, but production at the facility was not resumed.[184] In Alberta, Fritz Sick had transformed his modest first brewery into the Lethbridge Brewing and Malting Company, and by 1906 his beer was available in Fernie.[185] The Royal Hotel was alone in offering patrons Sick's brew locally, claiming it was "the only good beer in Fernie." For private consumption, the Pollock Wine Company of Fernie advertised its bottled American-made Schlitz beer, which then enjoyed Milwaukee's reputation for quality.[186]

Confident and profitable, the Fort Steele Brewing Company announced plans in the autumn of 1906 to expand its operation on Cokato Road. It called for tenders to construct a new fire-proof building of brick, steel, cement and stone, with the capacity to produce 30,000 barrels annually.[187] For over a year, further details of those plans were not made public, but the souvenir booklet published by the *Fernie Free Press* just before Christmas 1907 contained an advertisement, showing an architect's rendition of a strikingly modern facility. The illustration also indicated that other changes were being made. The company's lager beer was to be renamed Mutz's Extra, and the company itself would no longer be the Fort Steele Brewing Company at

RUINS OF THE FORT STEELE BREWERY THE FIRST BUILDING BURNT IN THE GREAT FIRE OF AUG 1 08 FERNIE BC PHOTO SPALDING.

Mutz (*on the right, with cap, mustache and bow tie*) and a work crew prepare to clear the debris, August 1908. Fernie & District Historical Society1358

Fernie; it had become the Fernie-Fort Steele Brewing Company.[188]

At the same time, it seemed other competitors were about to emerge—much closer to home. Mutz had not proceeded with his plans for a brewery at Blairmore, and others saw an opportunity. In the summer of 1907, hotelmen in the Crowsnest Pass announced the creation of the Blairmore Brewing and Malting Company.[189] On the British Columbia side of the border, plans were further advanced. Arrangements for the construction of a new brewery at Natal were all in place by the end of 1907. In charge would be none other than Otto Meier. The brewmaster at the original Fort Steele operation, Meier had accompanied Mutz on the move to Fernie, but left the company soon after it incorporated.[190] By coincidence or design, the contract for Mutz's new brewery on Cokato Road was awarded in May 1908—just as Meier's bottled beer from the Elk Valley Brewing Company first became available.

Mutz was a busy man. He was president of a new venture—the Fernie Brick Company—had increased his interest in the Coleman Hotel, and was supervising preparations for construction at Cokato Road.[191] The Mutz residence was moved to clear the site just to the south of the existing brewery where the concrete foundations were

Mutz (*far right*) and the work crew pause and pose to show work in progress.
Image courtesy Stan Sherstobitoff

soon being laid for the new one. But all preparations came to an
abrupt halt on the first day of August. Strong winds from the south
sent a raging forest fire along Cokato Road, and before the day was
out the entire business district of the city of Fernie was burnt to the
ground. The wooden Fort Steele brewery was the first building destroyed. Reports of losses incurred by the company varied significantly. The *Coleman Miner* stated the loss was $30,000; the *District
Ledger* gave a preliminary estimate of $150,000; the *Fernie Free Press*
reported a figure of $185,000, of which insurance would cover nearly
half.[192] Just two weeks later, in an apparent show of bravado, the Fort
Steele brewery was advertising for orders.[193]

Filling any orders it may have received would have to wait. The
debris of the destroyed brewery was cleared quickly and construction resumed on the new facility in mid-September. Despite inevitable delays during the winter months, progress was sufficient to
allow a test of the new brewing system in April 1909. To mark that
occasion, Mutz flew the flags of Great Britain, Germany, the United States, Sweden and Italy, to honour men the *Fernie Free Press* described as "the representatives of those several nations whose brain
and brawn had made this magnificent building possible."[194] Satisfied

with the test results, Mutz began commercial brewing in mid-June. All that remained was what would now be called relaunching the brand. When that occasion arrived, it proved to be the most spectacular commercial opening Fernie was ever likely to witness.

To celebrate the remarkable rebuilding of the city in just twelve months, Fernie mayor Sherwood Herchmer declared August 2 a holiday. Picnics, a baseball game and a grand banquet organized by the board of trade at the Waldorf Hotel were planned. Mutz also scheduled the official reopening of his brewery for that date. He sent hundreds of personal invitations, and placed notices in the Fernie newspapers inviting everyone to help mark the occasion.[195] According to newspaper reports, over the course of the afternoon, almost every man in Fernie accepted the invitation. Offered beer, sandwiches, frankfurters and a selection of cheeses—courtesy of the officially renamed Fernie-Fort Steele Brewing Company—guests enjoyed an occasion that would long be remembered. Some took a tour of what the *Fernie Free Press* called the "new monster brewery" and expressed their astonishment at its modernity and capabilities. Ongoing work on the malting and bottling facilities would reportedly bring total expenditure to nearly $300,000 on a facility capable of producing 125 barrels a day.[196]

However, it quickly became clear Mutz would be allowed no time alone in the spotlight. Liquor merchant John Pollock was president of the Fernie Board of Trade and a director of the Elk Valley Brewing Company. He advertised regularly as the agent for draught and bottled beer from Natal, but immediately after Mutz's grand reopening he placed small notes in both the *District Ledger* and the *Fernie Free Press* touting Elk Valley bottled beer as "even better than imported Schlitz," "the best beer made" and "always on tap at the leading hotels."[197] Mutz, busy re-establishing contacts with local hotels following the opening of his new brewery, may have thought Pollock's timing unkind, but he had a greater challenge to face. He was admitted to hospital in mid-August with a fever that was soon diagnosed as a case of typhoid, not uncommon in Fernie at the time.[198]

For several months, the Elk Valley Brewing Company had been quietly enjoying the local monopoly long desired by Mutz. With its considerable investment in the new plant on Cokato Road, the Fernie-Fort Steele brewery might have been expected to return to competition aggressively. It certainly had done so with its reopening and it soon distributed a calendar throughout the Kootenays, but there was no such follow up with newspaper advertising. Until the Fernie fire, the Fort Steele Brewing Company had advertised for a decade in both the *Cranbrook Herald* and *The Prospector*. As Fernie-Fort Steele, the renamed company did not resume that tradition. Nor did it advertise in two new publications, the *Michel Reporter* and the *Hosmer Times*, both of which carried weekly advertisements for the Elk Valley brewery. Regular Fernie-Fort Steele advertisements—surprisingly nondescript for a business needing to regain lost market share—began to appear in mid-September, but only in Fernie's two newspapers.

Although Mutz bottle openers were made available, the personal connection of the company's chief executive to its most popular product was not featured in regular weekly advertising. Fernie-Fort Steele lager, rebranded as Mutz's Extra in 1907, was not mentioned by name in newspaper advertisements, which resumed the rather bland product listing of "beer, porter and aerated waters" after the opening of the new brewery. Only in the calendar, the *Progressive Fernie* booklet of 1909 and the *Catholic Directory* of 1910 is Mutz's Extra specifically named and promoted in company advertisements.

Advertising content notwithstanding, the Fernie-Fort Steele and Elk Valley breweries were both thriving as the economic boom con-

Advertisement in *Progressive Fernie*, 1909. Fernie & District Historical Society DL-PF-1909-0155

tinued. Their success brought renewed interest in brewing from Blair-more. In the summer of 1911, a group of investors finally began work on the construction of the long anticipated brewery there.[199] Mutz was attending to his considerable personal investments throughout the region, particularly to his hotels in Frank and Coleman and the property at Blairmore, which was being described as a "significant mining property." He also purchased the Michel Hotel and became a substantial investor in the rival Elk Valley Brewing Company.[200] Mutz's Extra was being shipped as far as Saskatoon.

However, economic conditions were deteriorating significantly by 1912. Nationally, the decade known as the "Laurier boom" was over; locally, miners were fortunate if they were employed part-time. To much surprise, Mutz decided to move to a small rural community and abruptly curtailed his business activities in the coal-mining com-munities. He sold his recently acquired interest in the Michel Hotel and his long-held share of the hotel at Coleman. At Frank, he closed his hotel and transported as much of its contents and materials as was possible to Vulcan in Alberta, where he planned to build and operate a new hotel.[201] While he would retain his address on Cokato Road for some time, Mutz soon moved his family to Vulcan. He re-mained as president of the Fernie-Fort Steele Brewing Company, but relinquished his position as manager of the brewery.

With Mutz still at the helm, the company announced plans to build warehouses in Medicine Hat and Moose Jaw and adopted a fresh approach to advertising.[202] Identifying Mutz's Extra as the "best beer made in British Columbia," an advertisement in J.F. Spalding's *Official Automobile Road Guide* of 1913 marked the change. Advertise-ments for the Fernie-Fort Steele Brewing Company and for Mutz's Extra then appeared on every page of Jeffries and Co.'s *Southeast Koo-tenay Directory 1914*. In the *Fernie Free Press*, the company responded to the outbreak of war in Europe by urging readers of the newspaper not to "overlook our beer in the war excitement."[203]

In the *District Ledger*, eye-catching advertisements employing hu-mour began to appear in May 1915. Whether or not Mutz was involved in their creation is not known. They all contain minor problems in grammar, perhaps reflecting the imperfect command of English for which he was known. The same advertisements and some new addi-tions—with English usage largely corrected—were then featured in the *Fernie Free Press*:

Alexander the Great was a great man. He drank beer. Perhaps he would have been a greater man if he had not drunk beer, but you had better take no chances.

The Turks were once a great people, but they refused to drink beer—and look at them now!

The best safeguard against intemperance in strong drink is to cultivate a taste for that harmless and wholesome beverage—good beer—we make it.[204]

Just as the advertisements were appearing, Mutz abruptly stepped down as president of the Fernie-Fort Steele Brewing Company. In keeping with the local economy, the brewing industry was experiencing a prolonged period of decline. The Blairmore Brewing and Malting Company—finally ready to start production—went bankrupt in 1915. The Fernie-Fort Steele Brewing Company nearly followed suit. The company found it necessary to negotiate a sizeable mortgage, an undertaking that resulted in the disturbing realization that Mutz's brewery was in serious trouble.

A group of shareholders resorted to legal action and a scathing auditor's report for the calendar year 1915 quickly followed. It found confusion over ownership and valuation of properties listed as company assets in Moose Jaw, Medicine Hat and Cranbrook, and of hotels in Blairmore, Frank and Fernie. Although Mutz was not mentioned by name, the auditor complained of being hampered in his assessment by the "incompleteness, looseness, and general inadequacy of the records." Company directors declared an intention to continue production, but entered into voluntary liquidation—a form of creditor protection—in January 1916.[205]

Further depressing the industry, the adoption of prohibition by British Columbia a year later allowed breweries to produce only aerated waters and 2-percent beers.[206] Struggling through these years, the Fernie-Fort Steele Company nevertheless introduced its new Lion brand of low-alcohol beer and porter in 1917, and added to its range of aerated waters with the introduction of Orange-Kist and Lemon-Kist in 1920. At the same time, the sale of its interests in the Cosmopolitan

Hotel in Blairmore and the Royal Hotel in Fernie enabled the return to financial stability. Not all financial transactions appeared on the balance sheet, however. Rumours that the brewery continued to make and sell illicit beer were confirmed by a charge laid under the Prohibition Act in 1919. The brewery did not contest the charge and was fined $500.[207]

When prohibition in British Columbia ended in 1921, the company finally emerged from creditor protection and resumed its production of full-strength beer and porter, marking the occasion with a series of weekly advertisements urging *Free Press* readers to "Drink Fernie Beer."[208] The directors then made the surprising decision to stop advertising entirely after October 1921. The absence of advertising now makes it difficult to be certain, but it seems the Mutz's Extra brand was not revived. Perhaps reflecting the widespread post-war avoidance of overt Germanic associations, the flagship Fernie-Fort Steele brew was to be marketed simply as Fernie Beer.

Fernie Free Press, 28 October 1921, p. 3.

Mutz remained as a director and the company's largest shareholder. The objectives of management remained unchanged, and a singular opportunity was quickly recognized. Without a line of aerated waters, the Elk Valley Brewing Company had not survived the prohibition era. The Fernie-Fort Steele Company purchased the shuttered brewery in 1921 and closed the operation completely.[209] One newspaper commented astutely that the brewers of Cokato Road believed in "the judicious control of the output of the malt product."[210] The regional monopoly of production—so long desired, so long pursued—had finally been achieved.

No children or dogs were present for the final commemorative photograph, *circa* 1950. Fernie & District Historical Society 6664

Postscript

Albert Mutz remained a frequent visitor to Fernie, typically to attend board meetings of the Fernie-Fort Steele Brewing Company and the Fernie Brick Company, and also often en route to the United States. In 1918, one such journey was interrupted by ten days' detention at the Kingsgate border crossing, when American officials suspected his travel plans were connected to Germany's war effort. He remained on the board of directors of the Fernie-Fort Steele Brewing Company until his death in 1932.

The company then restructured, finally dropping "Fort Steele" from its name and acquiring what Mutz would have called a "branch brewery" in Cranbrook in 1933. The renamed Fernie Brewing Company marketed its "Beer from the Mountains" for the next quarter century. In 1950, the company amalgamated with Kootenay Breweries of Nelson to form Interior Breweries Limited.[211] In 1956, when Interior Breweries announced it would centralize production at Creston, the plan raised such alarm in Fernie that some civic politicians suggested banning the sale of Interior Brewing products within Fernie unless the local brewery remained in operation. However, the end of an era had clearly arrived. Production on Cokato Road ceased just as the first shipment of Fernie Beer—brewed in Creston—arrived in May 1959. The building once known as Mutz's brewery was gifted to the City of Fernie and demolished in 1960.

Photo Gallery

Fernie-Fort Steele Brewing Company promotional calendar, c. 1909/1910.

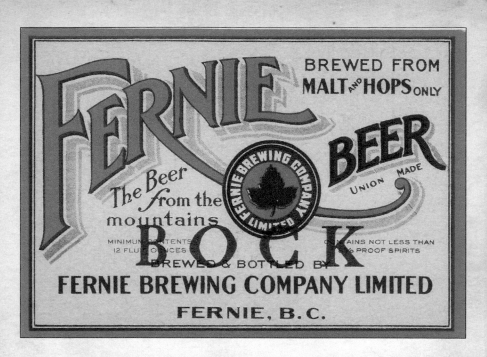

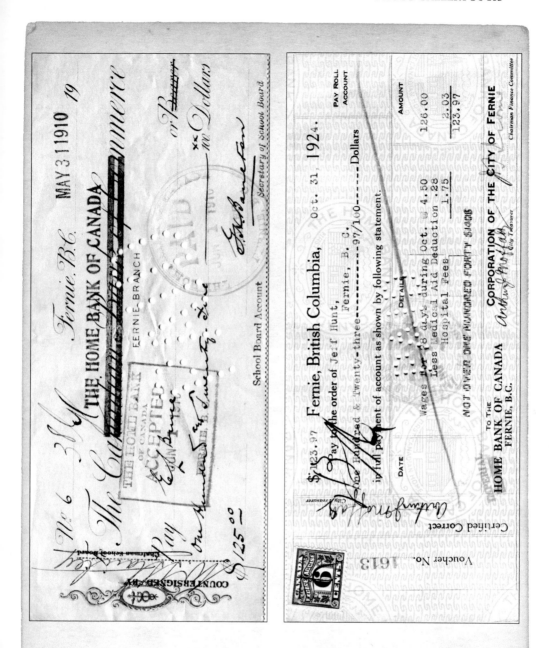

Images of the Home Bank of Canada five-dollar bill (above) and Fernie municipal cheques (page 103) courtesy of Ronald Greene.

Fernie-Fort Steele Brewing Company and Fernie Brewing Company colour images on pages 97-102 courtesy of the Fernie & District Historical Society, Stan Sherstobitoff and Wayne Norton. The Fort Steele Brewing Company Select Beer label (c. 1902) is from the first beer brewed and bottled in Fernie. It is included courtesy of the late Frank Mrazik."

"Solid and Managed with Rigid Conservatism"

The Home Bank Collapse of 1923

The city of Fernie is strewn with remembrances of a long-forgotten bank. The handsome building that once housed it has been refurbished and dedicated to other purposes; the streets bearing the names of its executives remain, though disguised by their modern numerical designations. Descendants of residents who lost their savings still speak of family difficulties resulting from a terse written notice, placed one fine summer's day nearly a century ago, on a closed bank door. The failure of the Home Bank of Canada is a story known in broad outline, but it is little understood that the consequences—both financial and psychological—were more deeply felt in Fernie than anywhere else in the country.

While the eventual story of the Home Bank in Fernie is calamitous, its early history—in two respects—is rather curious. In May 1906, the bank's general manager, James Mason, visited Fernie to make arrangements for the opening of a local branch. As a director of the Crow's Nest Pass Coal Company, Mason was well known in Fernie: after all, a street was named after him in the Annex. He announced—probably to the surprise of everyone—that Fernie was to be the location of the bank's first branch outside Ontario. At the time, the bank had been incorporated for not yet two years and all of its nine existing branches were in, or near, Toronto.[212]

The Fernie branch of the Home Bank was opened on the first day of August in modest, leased premises in the Henderson Block on Victoria Avenue.[213] To supervise a staff of three, J.H. Marshall left his position as cashier with the Crow's Nest Pass Coal Company to become manager. Fernie resident Joseph Rudnicki—in part because of his familiarity with eastern European languages—was hired as clerk. Regular advertising in Fernie's two newspapers began immediately.

Following the fire of August 1908, the Home Bank quickly re-established itself.
Fernie & District Historical Society 0186b

Participating in the community's resurrection following the great fire of 1908, the bank received vigorous applause when it announced an impressive building would be erected at the corner of Victoria Avenue and Cox Street.

Reported to be "solid and managed with rigid conservatism," the Home Bank was prepared nevertheless to take some risks. Amidst some confusion and concern at city hall about civic finances early in 1910, managers of local branches of Fernie's four banks were asked if better terms could be secured regarding the city's overdraft. Having acted as the city's financial institution for many years, the Canadian Bank of Commerce was reluctant, but the Home Bank offered an arrangement that would reduce overdraft costs by more than $1,000. In May 1910—to considerable surprise and without public explanation—the City of Fernie transferred all its accounts from the Canadian Bank of Commerce to the Home Bank.[214]

The new Home Bank building opened officially in March 1911, and regular advertisements continued to appeal particularly to depositors of modest means. Accounts of as little as $1 were actively solicited. Consequently, the bank was increasingly favoured by miners and their families. Following several managers of short tenures, J.F. Macdonald took over in September 1911. In charge for six years, Macdonald was promoted to take over the new "flagship" branch opening in Vancouver near the end of 1917. The personal popularity of his replacement, Alexander Watson, became a factor in attracting accounts from fraternal organizations, churches and other community groups.

District Ledger, January 8, 1910. UBC Library Open Collections: BC Historical newspapers

By the early 1920s, as a solid and well-established part of the community, the Home Bank in Fernie was second only to the main branch in Toronto for the amount held on deposit.

FRAUD IN TORONTO, FURY IN FERNIE

Repeating the norms of previous years, the financial report for the year ending May 31, 1923, was issued in Toronto by the Home Bank on June 30.[215] Signed by bank president Herbert Daly and general manager James Cooper Mason (son of James Mason), it showed a healthy balance sheet and stated that a quarterly dividend—one that would complete a 7 percent return to shareholders for the year—would be paid on August 17. Having received the same dividend in 1921 and 1922, shareholders had no reason to doubt their investments were secure. Depositors and local investors may have wondered why the usual weekly advertisement for the Home Bank—which had been included in each issue of the Fernie Free Press for so many years—was missing in July and August. Probably they did not.

The news arriving in Fernie after business hours on August 17, 1923, was not believed at first. How could the most trusted financial institution in town have shuttered its doors? Disbelief was strained when the bank did not open as usual at ten o'clock the next morning and evaporated entirely at eleven o'clock when a notice was posted on the door confirming the suspension of bank activity. As the *Fernie Free Press* soon noted, "Nearly every other man or woman in the city is tied up in some business relation with the Home Bank, which had the complete confidence of the local public." The newspaper's editor, John Wallace, gave high praise to the "efficient manner" in which the Fernie branch had been managed, claimed several chartered banks were already sending representatives to examine the possibility of locating in Fernie, and cited reports from Toronto indicating depositors would suffer little, if any, loss.[216]

It was soon apparent, however, that the atmosphere of relatively calm acceptance conveyed by the *Free Press* prevailed neither in Toronto nor in Fernie itself. To wrap up the affairs of the bank, a curator was quickly appointed by the Canadian Bankers Association; at the same time, the association denied all responsibility for losses incurred. The *Toronto World* newspaper was predicting depositors could expect only 64 cents on the dollar, but not until the end of November. In Fernie, many residents, fearing a wider banking crisis, had rushed to withdraw their savings from the Imperial Bank and the Bank of Commerce. They were soon reassured the crisis was evidently confined to only one institution, but Home Bank depositors remained deeply distressed. On the evening of August 30, approximately three hundred people attended a meeting called at the Grand Theatre by Mayor George Henderson.

George Gerrie Henderson was in his fourth year as mayor of Fernie. He was an established businessman, owner of the Henderson Block on Victoria Avenue, founder of the *Fernie Free Press*, a customs collector and a former school trustee. He arrived at the meeting in an angry mood and with four resolutions in hand. The first insisted that liquidation of the bank should be delayed until a full accounting of assets and liabilities was available; the second called upon the federal government to appoint an independent representative to work with the curator. The third called upon the Canadian public to withdraw all deposits from all chartered banks if Home Bank depositors received anything less than the full amount of their bank balances. If that was not enough to shock observers, the final resolution certainly was. It demanded that the federal government take over and operate Canada's chartered banks.

John Wallace at the *Fernie Free Press* gasped at the last two resolutions, noting they were grist for the mill of local Federated Labour

Party MLA Thomas Uphill. Mayor Henderson was generally known to be a Liberal in politics. He was not on the same political page as Thomas Uphill, and his anger was not derived from a comparable socialist critique of capitalist society. As mayor, however, he was fully aware that the City of Fernie had its accounts with the Home Bank and, like all other depositors, had no immediate access to them. Frozen were $25,000 in the sinking fund, $65,000 for current purposes and waterworks; $17,000 for a planned sewer extension in the Annex and $12,000 for an addition to the Central School. City finances were paralyzed.

George Henderson. Fernie & District Historical Society DL-PF-1909-0312

Those attending at the Grand Theatre supported Henderson's proposals enthusiastically. A committee of seven was appointed to refine the wording and forward the resolutions to the prime minister, the minister of finance, the Canadian Bankers Association and the curator.[217] In total, deposits of approximately $800,000 were estimated to be on the books at the Fernie branch, while bank shares nominally valued at between $10,000 and $20,000 were said to be held by local residents.[218] Anxious depositors and shareholders spent the month of September anticipating the report of the curator, which was delayed week by week.

News was received that organizations of depositors were forming across the country, and a committee emerged quickly in Calgary. Led by Herbert Higginbotham, secretary of the United Farmers of Alberta, the committee demanded full reimbursement, but otherwise adopted resolutions much milder than those approved at Fernie. Blairmore found itself in the same situation as Fernie, with its school board funds frozen alongside business accounts and savings accounts reportedly held by "427 miners, 69 children, and 102 women." On September 4, a well-attended meeting heard W.A. Beebe, vice-president of the Blairmore Board of Trade, urge his listeners to follow the lead of Fernie's depositors. Ignoring their counterparts in Calgary, the meeting in Blairmore adopted precisely the same resolutions introduced a week earlier by Mayor Henderson.[219]

The Royal Bank quickly announced it would locate a branch in Fernie, and there was speculation that Alexander Watson, whose reputation remained high, could be offered a position. When the new bank branch opened in temporary quarters in the Hotel Fernie on the first of October, Watson was indeed named branch manager. Regular advertisements for the Royal Bank featuring his name began to appear in the *Free Press* a week later. To replace Watson at the Home Bank, William Bird, while remaining manager at the Home Bank in Blairmore, also took charge of the branch in Fernie.[220] When the curator's report was released on October 3, precise figures for assets and liabilities were made public. The Fernie branch—with $782,701 on deposit—held by far the greatest amount in western Canada. With a population far greater and $386,999 deposited at its local branch, Winnipeg was a very distant second.[221]

The curator's report caused uproar nationally and locally. The liabilities of the bank were found to exceed assets by well over $2.3 million. The curator declined to "hazard an opinion" about what amount depositors could expect to receive; nor would he comment on whether criminal liability existed in the filing of fraudulent reports. Nevertheless, all directors of the Home Bank immediately faced charges pertaining to fraud. General manager James Cooper Mason had evaded the gathering storm by committing suicide in early August. Bank president Herbert Daly—described by *Saturday Night* magazine as "not a banker, but a promoter"—was said to be so ill his doctors were preventing all news and newspapers from reaching him at his summer home on Lake Simcoe. He died just three weeks later.[222]

Emerging details brought further outrage. One bank director also sat on the board of the Canadian National Railway, which withdrew $1 million just before August 17. Earlier in the summer, the Home Bank had appealed to the federal government for what would now be called a bailout. The appeal was not successful, but was an open secret in Toronto's financial circles. There was much speculation about how significant other last-minute withdrawals might prove to be. Anger was only slightly tempered with the announcement that the Canadian Bankers Association—as a charge against the assets of the Home Bank—had finally agreed to arrange financing sufficient to allow a payment of 25 cents on the dollar for depositors. Proofs of claim were to be submitted by the end of November.

The impact of the bank's failure was becoming clearer locally. The Knights of Pythias Lodge No. 31 and its associated Pythian Sisters, with all their funds at the Home Bank, declared "no further confidence" should be placed in Canada's banking institutions and urged all Knights of Pythias lodges to withdraw their savings from all banks. The Fernie Hockey Club, pleased to have finished the 1922 season with a profit of $300, regretted it could not access those funds. The Alberta League champion Blairmore hockey team found itself in the same situation.[223] The Masonic Lodge, the Crow's Nest Pass Coal Company and the Great Northern Railway preferred not to make public the extent of their losses, but the committee raising funds for a children's swimming pool in Fernie was known to have raised nearly $6,000.

In mid-October, Bernard Caufield, superintendent of the mines at Coal Creek, called a meeting of depositors at the Literary and Athletic Association clubhouse. According to the *Free Press*, the meeting drew someone from practically every family living at Coal Creek. In his introductory speech, Caufield noted that the community's deposits in any bank "represent meagre savings from wages earned in a hazardous occupation." He cited a statement made by the minister of finance in May that depositors in Canadian banks need have no fear about the safety of their deposits, and he wondered if perhaps all deposits should be withdrawn from all banks and placed in the post office.

Consequences of the bank failure for individuals were introduced into the public discourse for the first time as Caufield named and described the circumstances of three men known to him. Each had worked in the mines for more than fifteen years; each was disabled and unable to work; each had lost all his savings; one was the only support of his mother and sister. All Coal Creek depositors were urged to provide details of personal circumstances in letters to the East Kootenay MP, Dr. James Horace King, and MLA Thomas Uphill. Letters were also to be sent to prominent politicians requesting their support, and one to the minister of finance pointedly asking if his statement of May—that depositors in Canadian banks need have no fear about the safety of their deposits—was true. If response to the letter campaign proved unsatisfactory, depositors in other banks would be urged to put their savings in the Post Office. Organized runs on other banks were openly advocated, but a resolution on that point was not put to the meeting.[224]

Mayor Henderson convened a second meeting of Fernie depositors on October 22 only to offer "no cheerful news." The ensuing discussion brought scathing criticism of the Canadian Bankers Association and the federal government for ignoring clear indications of serious problems for so long. There were renewed calls for withdrawals and organized runs on other banks, and for the nationalization of all Canadian banks. Mayor Henderson agreed the city would have to borrow and raise tax rates to meet obligations. William Wilson, president of the Crow's Nest Pass Coal Company and a Home Bank depositor, spoke of "broken confidence" in the banking system; he also offered to assist personally individuals in the most straitened circumstances. Henderson was chosen to represent Fernie at a national meeting of depositors that was being organized to take place in Toronto on December 6. A representative from Coal Creek would also attend—with all expenses reportedly to be paid by "one generous individual"—and it was agreed that the Fernie and Coal Creek committees should act jointly in future. Finally, acknowledging that consequences were being felt not only by current and former coal miners, five women were added to the committee.[225]

At Coal Creek, too, there was also a follow-up meeting on October 25, but that gathering seemed less inclined to coordinate its efforts with the Fernie committee. Bernard Caufield accused Fernie residents of being "too dead" and lacking in energy in making demands for full compensation. He said Coal Creek residents—with two hundred depositors at the Home Bank from a population of just six hundred residents—would continue to strike hard with no fear of jail in the process. The Canadian Bankers Association was again singled out for particular criticism, and a proposal was adopted to place advertisements in British newspapers urging a halt to investment in Canada. John Smith, a former president of UMWA District 18, was elected as the Coal Creek delegate to the Toronto meeting.[226]

At Blairmore, a meeting of depositors on October 31 heard brief addresses from MP George Coote and MLA Philip Christophers before unanimously urging all workingmen and fraternal organizations to place their accounts with the Post Office until Canadian banks became more reliable and until Home Bank depositors received full reimbursements. The politicians and the mayor promised to do all they could to secure those conclusions. Because of its neglect, the federal government was held responsible. Clearly, the depositors of Fernie, Coal Creek and Blairmore broadly shared the same analysis of the cause of the bank failure and the same willingness to demand stern measures to achieve resolution of the problem.[227]

When Thomas Uphill arrived in Victoria on October 29 for the legislative session, he publicized the plight of his constituents through an interview devoted entirely to the local consequences of the Home Bank failure. He provided statistics and outlined losses to the Corporation of the City of Fernie, reported on the resolutions passed by the meetings at Fernie and Coal Creek, and justified them by concluding that the banks, as currently operated and supervised, "were a menace to the state and public welfare." Uphill followed the interview with a spirited speech in the provincial legislature on November 5, calling Home Bank officials "a bunch of pirates," but admitting it would do no good to see them in jail. Instead, he declared that if depositors did not receive full compensation, he would personally organize a plan to urge everyone in British Columbia to withdraw their savings from the banks.[228]

On the same day, a considerable number of people from Coal Creek did withdraw their savings from the Imperial Bank in Fernie. Dismissed by the *Free Press* as a naive run based upon anonymous "foolish rumours," the coordinated withdrawals were likely an expression of support by Imperial Bank depositors for their less fortunate Home Bank counterparts. Considering the actions proposed at the Coal Creek meetings, they may also have been acting to protest Premier John Oliver's recent assertion he would not urge the federal government to pay the depositors in full. It is even possible these withdrawals were intended to coincide with Uphill's speech on the matter in the legislature. William Bird soon announced he had accepted a position with the Sterling Bank in Saskatchewan, leaving long-time employee Joseph Rudnicki to conclude Home Bank affairs in Fernie.[229]

A Long and Winding Road

The meeting planned for December in Toronto generated both optimism and uncertainty. The governments of Alberta and Saskatchewan each appointed officials to represent depositors, but, perhaps because Vancouver branch depositors seemed resigned to their losses, British Columbia did not follow suit. Less than pleased with their government appointee, the Calgary association sent Herbert Higginbotham to speak for them. Also reluctant to leave their interests in the hands of the appointed provincial official, Blairmore depositors felt Fernie mayor George Henderson would better represent their interests. The situation at Blairmore—where the colliery had been closed for five weeks—mirrored that at Coal Creek, where the mines were working only two or three days a week. In each community, the bank failure damaged further a local economy already struggling.[230] On his way to Toronto, Henderson gave an interview in Calgary. He remarked he would call upon MP Dr. King, who had not yet replied to the letters sent from Coal Creek depositors in October.

As the representative for Fernie and Blairmore, Henderson was ex officio a member of the national executive that met at Massey Hall in Toronto on December 6. Because the Vancouver branch had not formed a depositors' association, Henderson, Higginbotham and a representative of the Winnipeg branch were alone in directly representing grassroots western interests. Joining them were the two appointees of the Alberta and Saskatchewan governments, dozens of representatives for Ontario branches, and—primarily from the Toronto region—approximately two thousand angry depositors. The discussion that followed the preliminary report from the liquidator was often raucous. Speakers were intent on expressing outrage and few were impressed that 25 cents on the dollar would be paid out before Christmas, noting the Canadian Bankers Association had only reluctantly allowed the liquidators to borrow sufficient funds against assets of the Home Bank to make that payment.

As a second, unofficial delegate for the Fernie branch, John Smith found little opportunity to address the meeting, but Mayor Henderson certainly did. Speaking on behalf of the Fernie and Blairmore branches—with their combined deposits approaching $1 million—and for the community of Coal Creek, he referred to "300 old men" from the mining communities, "broken-down, worn-out and now penniless." He appealed to the prime minister and every member of the House and Senate: "For God's sake, have a heart, and do not dump these old people to put in the few remaining years of their life in the poorhouse or in the most abject poverty."[231]

The Massey Hall gathering finally decided to focus on the goal of complete reimbursement and the need for a permanent committee to work toward that end. A resolution was passed urging the bank's approximately sixty thousand depositors to contribute half of 1 percent of the amount of their deposits to fund efforts on their behalf. Impressed by the evident abilities of Mayor Henderson, the meeting appointed him to the executive of a new organization: the Home Bank Depositors' National Relief Committee. Henderson was also selected as one of eleven inspectors charged with collecting the funds necessary to keep the committee operating.[232]

Once home in Fernie, Henderson made plans to report at a public meeting early in the new year, a meeting that MP Dr. King agreed to attend. First, however, came the Christmas payout. The new branch of the Royal Bank of Canada was almost overwhelmed by the number of people who came through its doors during the regular opening hours of Saturday, December 22. Paying 25 cents on the dollar to 360 Home Bank depositors who had filed proof of claim, bank manager Alexander Watson must have felt some degree of discomfort while greeting his former clients. Approximately $50,000 — most of it in small amounts — was paid out, followed by another $15,000 on the following Monday, Christmas Eve. While the Royal Bank in Calgary was also kept very busy, no rush at all was reported in Vancouver. The *Blairmore Enterprise* described the payout as a "consolation fee."[233] Precise figures are not available, but it seems reasonable to assume almost all depositors would have claimed the offered payment on, or soon after, December 22. For the 1,400 depositors at the Fernie branch, that meant at most $195,000; for Blairmore's 480 depositors, roughly $45,000.

By the end of the year, the basic facts about the history of the Home Bank were known and many more were revealed in the following months. It was not a tale of valiant struggle and noble failure; it was instead a saga of fraud and chicanery right from the start. The story began when the long established Home Savings and Loan Company of Toronto applied for incorporation as a bank in 1903. Investments made with loans by bank president James Mason to his friend Henry Pellatt were included in the new bank's capital base. Despite reservations held by the Department of Finance about solvency, the federal government — without any discussion in the House of Commons — granted the Home Bank of Canada incorporation in

1904. During legal proceedings two decades later, when asked when the Home Bank became insolvent, one chief justice replied, "When it was born." Because of the loans extended particularly to Henry Pellatt and the fraudulent accounting pertaining to them, historians would later agree.[234]

The Home Bank had expanded significantly prior to the Great War, opening new branches primarily in Ontario and Saskatchewan. When Sir Henry Pellatt (knighted in 1905) was completing his grandiose Casa Loma in Toronto prior to the war, he owed $4.5 million to the Home Bank. In 1914, the manager of the Winnipeg branch expressed his alarm over poor accounting practices to the bank's head office. His concerns were dismissed; he persisted, and eventually was fired. Management of the bank was transferred during the war from the Right Honorable James Mason (a senator since 1913) to his son, James Cooper Mason. Made aware of serious bookkeeping issues in 1915, 1916 and again in 1918, the federal minister of finance failed to take any meaningful action. Apparently encouraged, the bank opened its new "principal office" for British Columbia in 1917 in Vancouver. Ignoring the expressed concerns about its accounting practices and despite the post-war recession, the Home Bank in 1921 and 1922 established twenty-eight new branches. The Blairmore branch was one of them, opening in April 1921.

It was the end of operations for the Home Bank in 1923, but the road ahead for depositors would prove a very long haul indeed. The much anticipated public meeting to hear reports from Mayor Henderson and John Smith about decisions made in Toronto was scheduled for January 2, 1924, at the Grand Theatre. For the first time, Kootenay East MP Dr. James King was to speak publicly about the Home Bank failure. However keen MLA Thomas Uphill was to affect the situation, he was essentially powerless. Constitutionally, banking was clearly and completely within federal jurisdiction. The views held by Dr. King—a government MP and cabinet member—were much more consequential than those held by a provincial MLA.

At the last minute, Dr. King found obligations in Ottawa more pressing. He did, however, agree to attend a smaller gathering in Fernie city chambers on New Year's Day. Bernard Caufield pulled no punches in expressing his annoyance at the abrupt change of plan. Telling his MP that considerable arrangements had been made for him at the Grand Theatre, Caufield then outlined individual cases of distress at Coal Creek. He insisted bank officials "took our money and gambled with it." Mayor Henderson spoke along similar lines. Dr. King listened and promised to give "every consideration" to their concerns. Without Dr. King, the public meeting went ahead the next day with a disappointing number in attendance. John Smith praised Mayor Henderson for his participation at the Massey Hall event, while Henderson assured his audience the liquidators were reliable and would act "with no fear or favour."[235]

In civic affairs, Henderson was acclaimed as mayor for his fifth term, but the financial circumstances he and his aldermen faced were discouraging. Having claimed its 25 percent reimbursement in December, the city still had inaccessible funds of nearly $89,000 frozen with the Home Bank. To maintain operations, the first meeting of the new city council adopted the Temporary Loan By-law to allow borrowing of up to $57,000 at 6 percent interest from the Imperial Bank. Henderson's anger was as yet unabated. He said it was "a crime that such a by-law should have to be brought into effect," noting that the city would have shown a modest surplus if not for the "Home Bank steal."[236] An additional levy was soon added to school taxes and a Home Bank of Canada Deficit Account created to address the frozen civic funds.

There was some encouraging news when the federal government—accused of negligence by the National Relief Committee for failing to investigate Home Bank accounting practices in 1915, 1916 and 1918—ordered a commission of enquiry. At the same time, from Vancouver to Montreal, Home Bank branches were closing. In late January, the Fernie branch relocated from its grand building on Victoria Avenue to a much smaller office—located, with a certain degree of irony, on the ground floor of a building owned by and named after George Henderson. Announcing plans for considerable renovations, the Royal Bank purchased the vacant Home Bank building for $19,500 in April.[237] On the last day of May 1924, Joseph Rudnicki closed the doors of the Home Bank office in the Henderson Block for the last time. The *Free Press* noted it was sad to see the bank's "old servants turned out to rustle for new employment after giving the best years of their lives" to its service.[238]

As one of the inspectors appointed by the Toronto meeting, Mayor Henderson had taken on a role akin to that of a tax collector. By mid-January, he was pleased that the great majority of Fernie depositors had authorized liquidators of the Home Bank to pay the National Relief Committee one half of 1 percent of their deposits. Collections from Fernie amounted to over $3,000, just perhaps $900 short of the maximum possible. He was less than pleased that authorized payments from Blairmore were only $169 out of the more than $900 expected. In a letter to the *Blairmore Enterprise*, he told local depositors they had "not done their share" and held up "the little City of Fernie" as an example to follow. The criticism may well have been deserved, but it is unlikely the comparison was warmly received.[239]

Mayor Henderson suffered a personal loss with the unexpected death of his daughter in late May. At the request of the National Relief Committee, however, both he and Higginbotham soon found themselves back in Ottawa. The commission of enquiry was investigating the history of the bank, and, in the House of Commons, Calgary East Labour MP William Irvine and Macleod Progressive MP George Coote were calling for far-reaching reforms to the Bank Act. They spoke of the lack of oversight that allowed fraudulent statements from the Home Bank to go unchallenged for so many years, and were pressing the government for compensation for depositors. The revelation that a federal cabinet minister had withdrawn $4,000 in cash just hours before the bank closed its doors brought further pressure for action. In mid-July, the commission of enquiry found there had been "hopeless incapacity and wrong-doing" by the management of the Home Bank. It was the critical moment. The government accepted the report and acknowledged depositors had a "moral claim" to compensation. A payment—of an amount yet to be determined—seemed assured.[240]

Reporting to a meeting at the Grand Theatre at the end of July, Mayor Henderson acknowledged disappointment that the House of Commons took no action before adjourning, but otherwise reported in optimistic tones. Bernard Caufield expressed less optimism, and, with a year passed since the collapse of the bank, said he was tired of the delays. Nevertheless, he joined the others present in giving a hearty vote of thanks to Mayor Henderson, who received further praise in a letter from the chairman of the National Relief Committee for the significant role he had played in Ottawa.[241]

With a federal election widely anticipated, a rare opportunity to press Home Bank concerns soon presented itself. To a much greater extent than is the case today, the visit of a prime minister to a community in western Canada a century ago was cause for great excitement, and Prime Minister Mackenzie King's planned few hours in Fernie on October 28 proved no exception. In one of those hours he was scheduled to hear presentations about the Home Bank. Plans were made, speakers from Fernie and Coal Creek chosen, and a separate delegation from Blairmore was added to the agenda. Just as the visit was nigh, Mayor Henderson suffered a serious heart attack. If he was present at the meeting of depositors with the prime minister on the afternoon of October 28, his name does not appear in published reports.

Speaking on behalf of Fernie depositors at that meeting was William Wilson, president and general manager of the Crow's Nest Pass Coal Company. Opening his address, Wilson mentioned that "vindictive utterances" from Fernie were upsetting friends in Toronto, who thought them counter-productive. He sought to explain the anger behind those utterances through the extended metaphor of a river in flood that simply cannot be held back until the flood has run its course. His lengthy presentation acknowledged local distress, but then unexpectedly praised politicians for facing the difficult decisions they had to make. Many of those present would not have been expecting a political speech speaking so softly to power.

Wilson's speech was printed in full by the *Free Press*, but there are no reports of other presentations. MP George Coote spoke for Blairmore depositors, perhaps repeating the fact he had first mentioned in the House of Commons that fifty of them were schoolchildren.[242] Bernard Caufield probably repeated the case he had argued so frequently for depositors from Coal Creek, a case undoubtedly echoed by local firebrand Robert Draper from Cokato. It can be safely assumed that, collectively, they made it perfectly clear to the prime minister the river was still in flood. Mackenzie King's next stop was in Calgary, where he was informed there were 1,780 depositors in Alberta with $525,908 on deposit, and that amongst the depositors in Calgary were numerous women and children. To all arguments, whether they were softly spoken or otherwise, King replied with encouragement and a promise to introduce a measure in January when Parliament reconvened.[243]

Mayor Henderson was quickly up and about and travelled to Toronto in November for an executive meeting of the National Relief Committee, called to prepare for the anticipated legislation in the new session of Parliament. In mid-December he returned home, certain that the federal government would soon make a "substantial reimbursement" to Home Bank depositors. There must have been a feeling of déjà vu in Fernie where December 1924 seemed much like December 1923. Hope was on the horizon in the year ahead, yet the community was counting the costs: nearly $3,800 in interest was required from the city in 1924 on the loan from the Imperial Bank. Expressing vigour and optimism, Henderson announced he intended to seek the mayoralty once more. Completing the sense that everything old was new again, a bank was again in operation at the corner of Victoria Avenue and Cox Street. With extensive renovations completed, the Royal Bank of Canada had finally moved in. Any conflicting emotions manager Alexander Watson may have experienced were unrecorded.

At the last moment, Henderson decided not to seek the mayoralty in 1925. At his final council meeting, he outlined the considerable progress made by the community under his direction, and then retired from civic politics. However, if he thought his responsibilities concerning the Home Bank were also drawing to a conclusion, he was mistaken. There was no mention of the expected legislation in the Speech from the Throne in January. Declaring "the real time for execution of energy at Ottawa has arrived," the National Relief Committee once more summoned Henderson to Ottawa to assist with lobbying efforts during the new session of Parliament.[244] There he would remain for five months.

The National Relief Committee was becoming concerned for its own financial viability. Meetings in Toronto occasioned little expense for most executive members because their homes were there. However, travel and accommodation costs for lobbyists in Ottawa — especially for westerners Henderson and Higginbotham — were considerable. Costs of local committees, such as those in Fernie and Blairmore, were also covered by the national organization. The appeal for half of 1 percent had been generally successful, and Fernie in particular was known to have responded "almost to a man."[245] The committee was encouraged that depositors of the Vancouver branch, with the assistance of Higginbotham, were finally organizing. A Vancouver representative was added to the committee, and, in March, a letter arguing that success was nigh urged them all to sign the authorization. It ended bluntly: "Funds are needed. Do it now."[246]

The Home Bank building was purchased by the Royal Bank in 1924.
Fernie & District Historical Society 8917do

Hopeful of full reimbursement, the depositors were pressing for a payment of 60 percent from the federal government while also anticipating an eventual 10 or 15 percent from the liquidators. From the government, disappointment came quickly. Though much delayed, the bill finally found its way through the legislative process in June. The government intended to pay 35 percent to all depositors, but was forced to accept Senate amendments that reduced the funds being made available from $5.45 million to just $3 million and declared only private depositors with balances under $500 were eligible. Depositors with more than that amount were invited to appeal for a payment if "particular need" could be demonstrated, but no level of government, school board, fraternal organization, union, club, church or corporation would be eligible for a payment of any amount. The Home Bank Creditors' Relief Act, therefore, provided considerably less than anticipated for the majority of depositors, a complicated process of appeal with an element of hope for a minority, and no relief or hope at all for those in the excluded categories.

Although disappointed, the National Relief Committee must have been pleased that its lobbying efforts had resulted in an unprecedented action: no previous bank failure in Canada had ever resulted in government compensation. On the other hand, after two years of legal proceedings and an estimated expenditure of $500,000, all convictions of Home Bank directors and other officials were overturned on appeal. They were found not responsible for the circumstances that lead to the insolvency of the bank. The editor of the *Free Press* joined in the call for more rigid supervision of financial institutions and expressed the thought that must have been on everyone's mind: "We may well wonder just what it is a bank director is." The sense of justice denied would linger for years. The *Blairmore Enterprise* later commented on a three-year prison sentence given to a postal worker for stealing $4.75: "How does that punishment compare with that meted out to Home Bank directors?"[247]

With the government funds in hand, the liquidators issued a circular that was printed in newspapers across the country in late August and early September. "In the Matter of the Home Bank of Canada Payment to Creditors" identified in detail those eligible and those who were not; payments could begin in early September and were to be concluded by the end of June 1926.[248] The liquidators estimated that 80 percent of Home Bank depositors had funds of less than $500 in approximately 46,000 accounts nationwide. The settlement coincided with campaigning during a federal election, and when the matter of the Home Bank was raised at political meetings, Liberal candidate Dr. King managed to give himself credit for the passage of the bill. Oddly, without so much as a nod to the efforts of the National Relief Committee, the *Free Press* agreed.[249]

Under the Home Bank Creditors' Relief Act, twenty commissioners were appointed nationwide to deal with claims of over $500. As one of those commissioners, Henderson was responsible primarily for Fernie and Blairmore, and his main task became one of soliciting claims of "particular need." He frequently invited claimants to call at his office and travelled often to Blairmore. He was also getting impatient with cheques not yet claimed and with approximately seventy depositors whose claims were expected, but not yet submitted.[250] In his private life, Henderson was under considerable stress throughout this period, concerned that his eldest son had been confined as delusional to a private medical facility in New Westminster. However, the shock he had to bear in early December can hardly be imagined. Reported as a "double bereavement," news came from New Westminster of the death of his son on the same day his wife died in Fernie.[251]

The process of dealing with claims of over $500 was a complicated one. Claimants were required to provide full statements of their finances for the preceding three years. Supporting letters and affidavits were frequently necessary to verify those statements and to demonstrate that "particular need" existed. Henderson's task was to gather these documents and forward them to the judges of the exchequer court in Ontario who had been appointed to consider whether or not a claimant should be paid. Initially, the process worked well. Many of those with very substantial sums in their Home Bank accounts assumed they would not qualify and did not submit claims. However, as it became

> **TO HOME BANK DEPOSITORS**
>
> Mr. G. G. Henderson, of Fernie, will be in Blairmore Tuesday (tomorrow), December 22nd, for the one day only, to meet those who have not yet filed claims against the Home Bank.
>
> He will also have with him cheques for some of those who have already filed claims, and desires to deliver these personally to the claimants.
>
> There are some depositors at Coleman who have not yet filed claims, and they are urgently requested to do so at this time.
>
> Mr. Henderson will be at the Cosmopolitan Hotel on Tuesday.

Blairmore Enterprise, December 21, 1925. Peel's Prairie Provinces, University of Alberta

apparent that such claims were being granted, the number of claimants accelerated sharply just before the end of June 1926.[252]

Early in 1927, it became equally apparent that the available funds were insufficient. As a result, the judges were rejecting some claims while others of equal merit were accepted, yet some of those were paid only 15 or 20 percent. Complaints were accumulating, some of them from people who missed the June deadline. The National Relief Committee scheduled a series of meetings in Toronto to address the issue and summoned Henderson once more. He left Fernie in March, taking with him a sharply worded rebuke of a different nature from the editor of the *Free Press*. Wallace wrote that a statement from the liquidators was long overdue and implicated Henderson directly: "Are the liquidators and inspectors trying to make this Home Bank proposition a life job?"[253] In Toronto, the committee concluded it would require another $600,000 from the government to allow rejected and partially paid claims to be re-submitted and to allow all claims to be dealt with equally. Again the government provided encouragement, indicating it was receptive to the idea.

Once back in Fernie, Henderson continued to work on new and resubmitted claims. However, judging by occasional hints in his newspaper, *Fernie Free Press* editor John Wallace was not particularly impressed by those efforts. Wallace had been appalled at the resolutions Henderson took to the first local meeting of depositors in 1923 and then opposed the notion that Henderson might seek re-election in 1925. Whatever the cause of their personal antipathy may have been, the depth of the animosity Wallace and Henderson soon directed at each other in the pages of the *Free Press* must have surprised many readers. In December, Wallace alleged that one local depositor, having lost "the savings of a lifetime," received his payment only through the political efforts of local Liberals and MP Dr. King. Henderson responded that the payment, after several unsuccessful attempts, had finally been received, as he wrote, "through my efforts and mine alone." Wallace repeated his assertion and concluded: "We shall leave it to the public to judge." He also repeated his criticism of the liquidators: "Do these men consider they have a life job and that all the assets of the defunct institution are to be used for their expenses and salaries?"[254]

Neither man was content to let the other have the last word. Henderson challenged Wallace to prove his allegations, who in turn repeated the widely held belief that a local rich man had received his payment while poorer men were still being denied theirs; Henderson said he was sending the latest copy of the *Free Press* to the liquidators, presumably to see if statements it contained were libellous. Wallace asked why Henderson was defending "the silence of the liquidators." Anonymous letters to the editor followed, alleging Henderson's trips to Ontario were to "secretly knife his enemies, favour his friends, and lay the foundations for future political pull." There was criticism of the secret "Star Chamber proceeding" that determined who received a payment and who did not.

Finally, a letter from Bernard Caufield, as head of the "Unpaid Home Bank Depositors of Fernie," put an end to what he described as "scurrilous lying" about Henderson. He explained that a recent meeting gave Henderson a unanimous vote of confidence because his efforts on depositors' behalf had always been to their "entire satisfaction." Fifteen others joined Caufield in requesting that Henderson attend the next meeting in Toronto as their representative. The list of unpaid depositors included many well known in the business community—Carosella, Aiello, Bossio, Mills, Mangan, Ingram—presumably holders of unincorporated business accounts.[255]

Quite aside from their content, the series of letters inadvertently revealed two things: one was of national significance, and one concerned purely local detail. The inequitable treatment of depositors' claims as government funds ran down was causing considerable dismay by allowing misinformation and rumour to spread. The National Relief Committee was disappointed when the government committed only $200,000 in estimates for the new budget. To assist in pressing their request for more money, Henderson was again summoned to Toronto for meetings to begin the end of January 1928. The local revelation was contained in one of Henderson's letters to the *Free Press*. Of all the hundreds of claims he had submitted on behalf of depositors from the Fernie branch of the Home Bank, only twenty-three remained unpaid at the end of 1927.[256]

In Toronto, the National Relief Committee began to talk of winding up its affairs; it also reduced to $450,000 the amount it said would be required to complete final payments to Home Bank depositors. The delegation sent to Parliament Hill was much smaller than in earlier years: Henderson was one of only three designated to present the case for more funds to parliamentary caucuses and committees. Once there, doctors expressed renewed concerns about his health, but he insisted on continuing until the matter was concluded. By April, he was able to wire the news that the $450,000 would soon be approved. He returned in mid-May with cheques in hand for $14,800, belatedly drawn from what remained from the original $3 million allocation of 1925. Two weeks later, he was advised by MP Dr. King that when the estimates were passed in mid-June, $72,300 was earmarked for depositors from the Fernie branch.[257] Although there was no applause from the *Fernie Free Press*, Henderson must have enjoyed a deep sense of vindication.

Sadly, he had little time to revel in the moment. Preparing for a hunting trip in early September, George Henderson died of a heart attack. The obituary in the *Free Press* made scant reference to his years as mayor, but of his efforts in the Home Bank failure noted that he had "worked hard to recover the monies lost." It was left to his colleague Herbert Higginbotham to offer more fulsome praise. In a tribute published by the *Calgary Herald*, Higginbotham said Henderson was recognized as "a man of exceptional concentration of purpose" during the time he spent in Ottawa for the parliamentary sessions of 1924 and 1925. He said the judges of the exchequer court placed great reliance upon the diligence and impartiality he demonstrated while investigating literally thousands of claims. He added that Henderson's character was much admired by members of Parliament, but it was recognized that he returned to Fernie in May considerably run down in health.[258]

FINAL RECKONINGS

The death of Henderson in September very roughly concludes the story of the Home Bank and Fernie. But not quite. In mid-October, on behalf of the National Relief Committee, Higginbotham and John O'Reilly from Ontario visited Fernie. The years of preparing submissions to the court on behalf of claimants were over, but the need to distribute payments remained. The visitors appointed one of the yet unpaid depositors, John Mangan, vice-president of the Fernie Board of Trade, to complete that task for claimants from Fernie and Blairmore. Mangan was soon at work. Just one week later, he received approximately one hundred cheques for distribution to depositors with claims under $500. Most of these were likely for only small amounts, but in the difficult economic conditions of the 1920s, many single men and many families had left the region, some without providing forwarding addresses. Early in 1929, Mangan issued a notice that he still held three dozen of those cheques, and, if unclaimed by the end of February, they would be returned to the liquidators.[259]

· That ended the matter for local claims of under $500, but the settlement of claims over $500 was not yet complete. Mangan received thirty new cheques in January amounting to $17,500 and a further $9,000 in May. These were the final amounts expected in Fernie and Blairmore. At the post office, Mangan put up notices of the names of individuals for whom he had received cheques. Across the country, while the few remaining depositors under $500 were by then receiving cheques mailed from Toronto, cheques for depositors over $500 were still to be delivered personally by the local inspector. Probably all of the twenty-three unpaid individuals mentioned by Henderson in December 1927 received their 35 percent payments by hand from Mangan in May 1929.[260]

The depositor ultimately suffering the greatest loss in dollar terms was undoubtedly the still hopeful City of Fernie. Between 1924 and 1929, successive councils applied funds from general revenue surpluses and school levies to reduce the Home Bank of Canada Deficit Account from just under $89,000 to only $3,800. However, with high costs of relief and unpaid taxes, civic surpluses of the 1920s turned to deficits beginning in 1930. The possibility remained of a final 5 to 10 percent payment from the Home Bank liquidators, and, anticipating such a dividend would more than cover $3,800, the city made no further appropriation to reduce the Deficit Account. Finally, in January 1933—a decade after the bank's collapse—the liquidators announced that, due to depressed real estate prices, sale of the remaining assets of the Home Bank would not support a final payment to depositors. The announcement can have surprised no one, but was a final blow to all depositors and to the City of Fernie in particular. When the city went into public administration in January 1935, losses resulting from the bank collapse of 1923 were still a burden to civic finances.

In the absence of precise figures, it can only be estimated how much money was returned to depositors of the Fernie branch. Practically all depositors claimed the 25 percent offered in December 1923. Collectively, that would have brought them $195,000. The 35 percent offered through the Home Bank Creditors' Relief Act brought approximately $175,000 by the end of 1927. Successful appeals and the additional funding of 1928 saw probably a further $75,000 returned to the community, almost all of it for individuals with over $500 in deposits. By such calculations, Fernie depositors retrieved $445,000 over the nearly six years following the collapse of the Home Bank. Losses, therefore, were approximately $335,000.

Even more difficult is a consideration of how much was not recovered by each depositor. Certainly, everyone lost at least 40 percent. Private individuals with large deposits initially seemed likely to suffer losses of 75 percent, but eventually did receive the same percentage in reimbursement as those with smaller deposits. The community organizations, clubs, societies and governments suffered greater percentage losses. They received nothing further after the original 25 percent payout of December 1923. At Blairmore, the school district could not recover $7,000, but the amount collectively lost by the community as a whole can only be guessed at. The situation for individual depositors at the Blairmore branch was comparable to those at Fernie. If the same rough estimates of percentages are applied, losses in Blairmore were perhaps in the range of $75,000.

The Home Bank of Canada was not the first bank to fail in Canada, but it was the largest and it was the last. Changes to the Bank Act in 1924—introduced specifically in consequence of the Home Bank fiasco—imposed greater governmental scrutiny of banks and required of them a higher standard of accounting practices. The payout of government funds to depositors—stretching over more than four years—remains unique. So, too, does the experience of Fernie in the aftermath of the collapse. Considered together, the exceptional amount of money on deposit, the radical expressions of outrage, the prolonged involvement of George Henderson, and the heavy losses incurred by the civic government create a story that has no equal in the many other communities also stung by the bank's collapse.

POSTSCRIPT

It is unlikely that people walking by the Henderson Block on Victoria Avenue or by the museum at the corner of Victoria Avenue and Cox Street today will give a thought to long-forgotten individuals and financial institutions. Residents know that streets in Fernie were named to honour the original backers of the Crow's Nest Pass Coal Company, but may not be aware that two of the men so honoured—James Mason and Henry Pellatt—were primarily responsible for the financial crisis that struck the community so forcefully in 1923. Visitors to the museum might be surprised to learn they are standing in the building that was originally the Fernie branch of the Home Bank of Canada. Although a century has passed, whispers and echoes can yet be heard.

"LEE SOMETHING-OR-OTHER WAS HIS NAME"

CHINESE IMMIGRANTS AND THE FERNIE NEWSPAPERS

Ethnicity mattered in the early twentieth century. No accident or death at Coal Creek could be reported in local newspapers without the ethnic origin of the injured or deceased being mentioned; no crime or trial described without identifying victim or perpetrator as Italian, Slav, Swede, an American of colour—whatever the particular case may have been. Whether or not that alone reflects a racist outlook on the part of Fernie's residents of British origin (whose surnames in print required no additional word of ethnic identification) depends perhaps upon the definition of racism being considered. However, toward "Japs, Chinks and Hindoos," there can be no doubt that a racist perspective—one typically shared by the Italians, Slavs and Swedes—was an attitude broadly held within the community at large. Of the three Asian ethnicities, it was the Chinese who bore the greatest burden of that attitude.

The widespread animosity toward Chinese immigrants in Canada's Pacific province has been well documented by historians. Because of a lack of source material for Interior communities, the focus of most studies has been on the major population centres of Vancouver and Victoria.[261] Yet almost every town and village in the province became home to Chinese immigrants. The communities of the Elk Valley—from Elko and Morrissey to Hosmer and Michel/Natal—were no exception. Little can now be discovered about the immigrant experience in the smaller locations, but in the regional hub of Fernie, the local newspapers provide an uncomfortable insight into what the nature of that experience must have been.

Chinese men began to arrive in Fernie immediately the community was founded. Lee Bing Foon, who arrived in Canada in 1893, came to Fernie in 1898 and likely found work at the laundry just established at the corner of Baker Avenue and Cox Street. Jong Sam arrived in Canada as a labourer in April 1899 and by December was employed in Fernie as a cook at the Victoria Hotel. On Baker Street, which was soon described by the local newspaper as "Chinese headquarters," a store was also established before the turn of the century.[262] The cost of construction of the two buildings housing the laundry and the store was recorded as $900, an indication that the business owner intended to establish himself in the community. Other hopeful entrepreneurs soon followed suit. Both the Yee Lee and the Wing Kee laundries are listed in *Henderson's British Columbia Gazetteer and Directory 1900–1901.*

As was generally the case throughout British Columbia, the Chinese immigrants who came to Fernie were not viewed as integral and welcomed members of the community. During the first May 24 celebration in 1900, a hundred-yard "Chinamen's Race" was on the program, perhaps an attempt at inclusion, perhaps for intended comic effect. At the same time, a local police officer was found guilty of extorting $2.50 monthly from each of the four established Chinese businesses for what he claimed was "ground rent for Government land."[263] Stephen Wallace, who employed Chinese labour at his Fernie Hotel, announced he was seeking white workers from Winnipeg to replace them because he believed Chinese immigrants were "a detriment" to the country.[264]

The owner and editor of the recently established *Fernie Free Press* did not hesitate to make his views on race perfectly clear. George Henderson would also rage against "Slavs, Doukabors and Dagos," but he directed most of his anti-foreigner commentary against Chinese immigrants and frequently reprinted anti-Chinese news items from other newspapers. In editorials, he insisted: "The Chinaman is and always will be an undesirable element in this country..." and "[He] is an isolated, peculiar creature, who merely exists where a white man would live... and sends his earnings, when he is not in bondage, back to China..."[265] Henderson was perfectly in step with the *Cranbrook Herald*, which called for a boycott of all Chinese businesses in July 1900, and he applauded when citizens in Moyie reportedly rid their community of its thirty Chinese residents in February

THE DEPARTMENT OF THE INTERIOR.

CHINESE IMMIGRATION BRANCH.

C. I.
9

No. 24789

JUN 2 1915 191

To the Collector of Customs,
Port of **Vancouver**

I hereby give notice that I desire to leave Canada with the intention of returning thereto. I propose to sail or depart from **Vancouver** for **Hong Kong**.

on the **MONTEAGLE** day of **JUN 2 1915** 191

I intend to return to Canada at the port of **Vancouver**

I request registration and I attach my photograph hereto and give the following information for the purpose of my identification on my return.

My proper name is **Lee Bing Foon**

I am sometimes known as

I first came to Canada in the year **1893 (Van. Emp of Japan) June**

My place of residence in Canada is **Fernie B.C.**

Where I have resided since the year **17 yrs**

Certificate of Registration Form C. I. 5 No. **11273**

My present occupation is that of **Laundryman**

My place of birth was **Chin Sen Toon**

My present age is **43**

Height **5** feet **3** inches.

Facial marks or other peculiarities :—

**Mole above right eyebrow.
Two large scars left side neck
Two scars left forehead.**

I am personally known to **Wing Sang.** and

both of **Vancouver** to whom I would refer you for correctness of statements herein made.

坤 炳 李
(Signature of Chinese Person.)

I have personally examined the person of Chinese origin who claims to be the person above described and whose photograph is affixed hereon (2), who returned to Canada on the **Monteagle** day of 191 and declare him to be the same person.

C. E. Nelson
(Controller.)

Lee Bing Foon, one of Fernie's original Chinese residents, visited China in 1915 and returned to Canada—but not to Fernie—in 1920. LAC, RG 76, Immigration Branch, Immigrants from China, 1889-1949

THE DEPARTMENT OF THE INTERIOR.

CHINESE IMMIGRATION BRANCH.

No. 27232

Dec 13th 1916

To the Collector of Customs,

Port of Vancouver

I hereby give notice that I desire to leave Canada with the intention of returning thereto. I propose to sail or depart from Vancouver for Hong Kong on the Empress of Japan. day of DEC 14 1916 191

I intend to return to Canada at the port of Vancouver

I request registration and I attach my photograph hereto and give the following information for the purpose of my identification on my return.

My proper name is Ow Sing Lee

I am sometimes known as

I first came to Canada in the year 1900 (Van Em India) mar

My place of residence in Canada is Fernie B.C.

Where I have resided since the year 1900

Certificate of Registration Form C.I.5 No. 36 06660

My present occupation is that of Cook

My place of birth was Hoi Gan

My present age is 38

Height 5 feet 2¼ inches

Facial marks or other peculiarities:— Scar en cor mouth Raised mole & cu back neck Pit front R ear

I am personally known to Hin Ho Co and

both of Vancouver to whom I would refer you for corrections of statements herein made.

利 李 區

(Signature of Chinese Person.)

I have personally examined the person of Chinese origin who claims to be the person above described and whose photograph is affixed hereto (2), who returned to Canada on the Emasia day of 191 , and declare him to be the same person.

C. E. Wilson (Controller.)

Dated at 191

[OVER.]

Ow Sing Lee spent sixteen years in Fernie before returning to China in 1916. LAC, RG 76, Immigration Branch, Immigrants from China, 1889-1949

1901 by refusing to buy from, sell to or employ them. He asked why Fernie should not try the same plan to rid itself of "sixty of these undesirable aliens."[266]

That call having failed, he then alleged that vegetables from the Chinese gardens established in the spring of 1901 just south of Coal Creek threatened public health because of unsanitary practices.[267] Although ownership of the *Free Press* soon passed to others, the generally hostile tone set by Henderson was retained. New editors immediately pressed the theme of questionable sanitation—this time in connection with the hand laundries. The practice of expelling water from mouths onto clothes was found repellant, and an article reprinted from *Outlook* magazine alleged: "They boil clothes from brothels, from themselves and from their respectable customers in the same boiler."[268]

Henderson's estimate of the number of local Chinese residents was inflated, as the Canadian census conducted in April 1901 would soon reveal. The census provides a fascinating snapshot of a brand-new community. Located on the banks of the Elk River, Fernie was growing quickly to serve the interests of the Crow's Nest Pass Coal Company. The townsite was attracting professional men, entrepreneurs and, of course, workers for the new mines at nearby Coal Creek. The coal miners came primarily from the British Isles, the United States, eastern Canada, and—in surprising numbers—from the Austro-Hungarian Empire. The census also confirms the presence of three dozen Chinese residents, pioneers of an immigrant community offering to provide essential services to residents.

The Chinese residents were all male, and were recorded in the census as either Buddhist or Confucian in religion. The oldest was forty-two years of age, and none had come to Canada before 1886. Names that would be familiar locally for years to come are first found in the census. How Foon and Jing Wing are identified as heads of laundries, while Tom Lee had established a store selling Chinese merchandise. Business operators are typically identified as "Heads" in the census, while their employees are designated as "Lodgers." According to the census, all those designated as lodgers were working as laundrymen or cooks. While few specifics about work locations are available, the census does record that one cook was employed at the hospital, while two were employed at local brothels. Several were identified as working at hotels, including the Hotel Fernie, Stephen Wallace's attempt to secure non-Chinese labour apparently having failed.

There are clear indications that a mutual accommodation was being reached. The hand laundries were well patronized and their number was increasing; produce from the Chinese gardens found a ready market; employment opportunities as laundry and kitchen workers were plentiful in local hotels and lumber camps. When the mining disaster at Coal Creek in 1902 left so many families destitute, Chinese residents contributed over $50 to the relief fund. The largest contributions came from the business owners Wing Kee, Kwong Wo Yuen, How Foon, Tai Ching and Kai Ming, but modest amounts came from more than a dozen others. When a fund was launched to maintain a fire brigade in 1903, How Foon (who would soon begin advertising his "China Goods" in the *Free Press*) and Tai Ching each contributed $10. In their third year of operation, the gardens to the south of town received high praise from the *Fernie Free Press*, and when another newspaper, *The Ledge*, was established in Fernie in 1904, its first mention of the local Chinese community was a compliment to one Chinese cook for the artistry he displayed in creating a Christmas cake.[269]

One consequence of living in a shared community was welcomed by no one. In April 1904, a fire destroyed a six-block section in the centre of town—almost the entire commercial district. "Chinese headquarters" on Baker Avenue was completely destroyed. Losses suffered by Lee Gee and Wan Lee (both of whom carried no insurance) were $500 and $300 respectively. Insurance covered half of Wing Kee's $800 loss, while the two most prosperous businessmen, How Foon and Tai Ching, each suffered losses of $1,500 after insurance. All of the business owners quickly began to rebuild.[270] However, like the shabby, rebuilt hotels and shopfronts of their neighbours, the appearance of the new Chinese laundries and stores was less than impressive. One commentator soon described Baker Avenue as "only a collection of shacks with Chinamen standing in front."[271]

Another unwelcome shared consequence specifically affected poorer members of the community. Soon after incorporation, the City of Fernie imposed an annual $2 "road tax" on all male residents between the ages of twenty-one and fifty who did not hold a business licence and who did not otherwise pay civic taxes. Miners making perhaps $3 a day were unhappy, but labourers earning much less while working for How Foon and his fellow businessmen were distraught. A visit from city police was required in August 1905 to collect the tax from thirty-three reluctant Chinese residents, some of whom were reportedly found hiding under their beds. It was the first of what became an annual visit/roundup/raid by civic officials and an unsuccessful attempt at avoidance by Chinese labourers.[272]

Unlike some communities in British Columbia, Fernie generally avoided anti-Asian laws and covenants. There were no restrictions on property ownership, school attendance or cemetery burials. The only exception was the prohibition of "spitting water from the mouth on laundry," which was included in the City of Fernie's first and subsequent health bylaws. However, the fact that fines were imposed on only three individuals—Sim Foon in 1905; Lee Long and Lee Hong in 1909—suggests city police and the community at large were little concerned with enforcement on the matter.[273]

Accepted however reluctantly as cooks, laundrymen, gardeners and members of the business community, the Chinese found no such acceptance in the coal industry. In its employment practices, the Crow's Nest Pass Coal Company (CNPCC) initially did not follow the example set by the collieries on Vancouver Island, where Chinese labour exerted significant downward pressure on wages paid to non-Chinese miners. Coal magnate Robert Dunsmuir regularly urged that cheap labour be made available to industry in general. In his own coal operations on Vancouver Island, approximately 25 percent of his employees were Chinese in the first decade of the century.[274] After its first few years of operation, the CNPCC did decide to experiment with the Dunsmuir model, employing Chinese labourers at the tipple in Michel and at the coke ovens in Fernie in 1903.

The experiment was short-lived. At Fernie, Chinese workers were provided by a labour contractor to work at the coke ovens. Acting together, the workers soon all quit. According to one report, the CNPCC found them unsuitable and employed immigrants from eastern Europe who were also willing to accept comparably low wages. Another report proffered Chinese superstition for their collective departure, stating they saw "devils in the flames" at the coke ovens. However, just before the change in personnel, four men assaulted one of the Chinese coke-oven workers and robbed him of $59, probably the sum total of what he had so far earned. It may well be the "devils" seen in the flames represented the possibility of ongoing harassment by displaced British workmen.[275]

Tempted to emigrate by attractive wage rates, experienced British coal miners found that the harsh living conditions and high costs of living in the Elk Valley accompanied those wages. They were concerned that immigrants from the peasant societies of Italy, eastern Europe and China—with no tradition of trades unionism—were willing to work for lower wages, and that their employer seemed increasingly eager to engage them. When the United Mine Workers of America (UMWA) organized District 18 in 1903, it addressed this concern by specifically inviting all European immigrants to join the union. However, no such invitation was extended to Asian-born workers. Article 1 of the District 18 constitution, apparently intended to express principles of solidarity, contains a specific and contradictory exception. The article appealed to "all men (except Chinese and Japanese) regardless of race or color to unite with the union to improve the material, intellectual and moral condition of the toilers in and around the mines."[276]

By contractual agreements with District 18, the CNPCC agreed not to employ Chinese or Japanese workers in underground positions, but retained the right to do so in above-ground occupations. Although mining companies at Coleman, Bankhead and Canmore did employ Chinese labour, after 1903 the CNPCC did not. Always concerned the company might change that policy, the union soon adopted a different defensive tactic. Believing the CNPCC would have no interest in employing Asian labour if required to pay union wage rates, UMWA District 18 deleted "except Chinese and Japanese" from its constitution in 1909.[278] Whatever the tactic and whatever its effect, the threat to wage rates posed by cheap Chinese labour was ever only an imagined danger for miners at Fernie.

Asian labour in general received constant attention in the Fernie newspapers, but specific references to local Chinese residents are remarkably few. An occasional compliment to a Chinese cook, a couple of advertisements placed by Chinese merchants, and a few warnings about the dangers of employing cheap labour indicate a community attitude parallel to that presented by newspapers throughout the province. While *The Ledge* was published in Fernie, editor Robert Lowery did not hesitate to criticize "crooked and incompetent" mine and mill owners for employing cheap Japanese labour, on one occasion damning a mill owner at Salmo for allowing Swedish lumbermen to remain out of work "while the yellow boys saw the wood."[279] His animosity towards Asian immigrants was evident in almost every issue.

THE DEPARTMENT OF THE INTERIOR.

CHINESE IMMIGRATION BRANCH.

No. 24788

JUN 2 1915 191___

To the Collector of Customs Vancouver
Port of _____

I hereby give notice that I desire to leave Canada with the intention of returning thereto. I propose to sail or depart from Vancouver for Hong Kong.
on the MONTEAGLE day of JUN 2 1915 191___
I intend to return to Canada at the port of Vancouver _____

I request registration and I attach my photograph hereto and give the following information for the purpose of my identification on my return.

My proper name is Lee Gee Choy.
I am sometimes known as _____
I first came to Canada in the year 1912(Via. S.S. Inaba Maru)Dec.
My place of residence in Canada is Fernie B.C.
Where I have resided since the year 3 yrs
Certificate of Registration Form C. I. 5 No. 75268.
My present occupation is that of Student
My place of birth was Chin San
My present age is 17
Height 5 feet 4 inches.
Facial marks or other peculiarities :—
Scar centre forehead
Mole top left neck
Mole near right corner mouth.

I am personally known to Wing Sang and
both of Vancouver.
of statements herein made. _____ to whom I would refer you for correctness

I have personally examined the person of Chinese origin who claims to be the person above described and whose photograph is affixed hereon (X), who returned to Canada on the 6th Kiana
day of _____ 191___, and declare him to be the same person.

Dated at _____ , 191___

[OVER.]

Identified as a student, Lee Gee Choy had lived in Fernie for three years when he returned to China in 1915. LAC, RG 76, Immigration Branch, Immigrants from China, 1889-1949

After Lowery moved to Nelson in 1905, his former newspaper became first the *Fernie Ledger* and then the *District Ledger*, soon after it was purchased by UMWA District 18 in 1907. Editors generally avoided the sharp tones of Lowery when commenting on Asian immigrants, but continued to express concern about Japanese labour, especially when a small number of Japanese labourers were employed for a few days at the coke ovens at Fernie in 1907.[279] That same animosity was less frequently expressed, but just as clearly, in the pages of the *Free Press*, which warned of the negative impact of employing "Hindoo" (who were typically Sikh sawmill workers), Chinese and Japanese labourers. The *Free Press* did not condemn the rioters at Vancouver in 1907, commenting only that "anti-Asiatic feeling at the Coast is manifesting itself about 25 years late."[280]

Perhaps predictably, the question of employing Asian labour locally found its focus in the Chinese laundries. As the number-one need in civic improvements—ahead of a library, a curling rink and street lighting—editor George Pedlar at the *Free Press* began to insist the establishment of a steam laundry was "the crying need of Fernie," so the choice for residents could then become "Steam Laundry or Chink."[281] At the *District Ledger*, William Stanley took over as editor early in 1908, and he immediately adopted the issue as his own.

The opening of the Fernie Steam Laundry in February 1908 was welcomed by both the *District Ledger* and the *Free Press*. Proclaiming "Joyful News to All White Men," the first advertisements for the new laundry in both newspapers announced that only white labour would be employed. Stanley urged his readers to "Cut out the Chinks, and patronize the White Man's laundry." He visited the new facility, applauded its modern methods, and noted: "All clothes are thoroughly disinfected... That is something your Chinaman will not do." He urged Fernie citizens to show their appreciation "by completely cutting loose from the Chinks and sending their washing to the Fernie Laundry."[282]

Stanley's initiative had an immediate effect in the broader community. As a member of the Fernie Board of Trade and soon as chairman of the school board, Stanley was an influential voice in local affairs. Early in 1908, the Royal Hotel (owned in part by Fernie mayor William Tuttle) began to advertise that it employed only white help, while the Fernie Steam Laundry continued to emphasize its employment policy throughout the summer, urging *District Ledger* readers to "Get the Chink smell off you by calling 135." Exploiting the widespread concern about scarlet fever, the laundry asked: "Worried about Scarlet fever? There is no wonder when you send your laundry work to the dens of the unsanitary Chinks."[283] In editorial notes, Stanley repeatedly echoed the laundry's advertisements, on one occasion noting the Chinese were prone to diseases of horrible character; on another, urging business owners not to patronize "the almond eyed, five cent a day Chink."[284] In July, the Queens's Hotel announced that henceforth it too would employ only white help.

The fire of August 1908 put an immediate halt to the laundry question and to every other matter of civic importance. The entire commercial district was devastated, and, for the second time in just four years, every Chinese-run business was destroyed. Unlike the more inclusive newspaper coverage of the 1904 fire, no indications of the financial losses suffered by Chinese businesses were published. However, reconstruction was soon underway. Like almost every other prominent Fernie businessman, How Foon announced he would continue to operate in a temporary structure, while undertaking to rebuild in brick and stone for a bigger and better Fernie. More modestly, the several smaller Chinese stores and laundries also began to re-establish themselves, some on Baker Avenue, but most toward the northern end of Victoria Avenue. "Chinese headquarters" was dividing into two, making it impossible after 1908 to refer to a single Chinatown in Fernie.

Even as rebuilding was just getting underway, Stanley returned to his theme, urging the owner of the steam laundry to reopen to help rid the city of "some of our measly almond eyed chinks."[285] In February 1909, when a cooks' union was formed and admitted to the Trades and Labour Council, Stanley wrote: "It is up to the union men of the city to compel hotel proprietors to hire union cooks and rid the city of the Chinks." Apparently responding to that call, men at the boarding house in Coal Creek announced their new cook was English after they had "sent another Chink cook about his business." At the same time, the International Brotherhood of Teamsters local union announced it would fine any of its members found to be patronizing Chinese or Japanese cooks at establishments where white cooks could have been employed.[286] In May, Stanley criticized his neighbours for employing Chinese workers in their gardens. The Chinese, he argued, can live on 10 cents a day and send their money home to China, but a white man spends his in the community. Residents, therefore, "should turn down the Chink, and engage a white man, and make this a white man's city." Effectively, Stanley was renewing Henderson's call of 1901 to rid Fernie of its Chinese residents.[287]

The *Fernie Free Press* also commented on the employment of Chinese gardeners, noting "We want a green Fernie (lawns, trees, etc.) but a white BC."[288] When the steam laundry was re-opened, the newspaper ran the headline "Exit Chinks, No More Washee" and advised readers: "The day of yellow odorous linen and tub-frayed garments will soon be a memory."[289] At the same time, editor George Pedlar had become more interested in matters surrounding gambling and opium use. A recurrent theme in the experience of Chinese men living in Fernie was the attempt to suppress their gambling and drug use. The first reported police raid occurred in March 1905, just after incorporation. How Foon, the Chinese community's leading businessman, was charged with selling opium at his restaurant. The charge against Foon was soon withdrawn, alleged instead against Yip Sing (the restaurant manager), and subsequently dismissed in court.[290]

No further raids were reported for several years, but the lull ended spectacularly in 1910. An anonymous letter from a Chinese resident, written in broken English and complaining of unfair prosecution of gambling, was published in the *Free Press* and taken by Pedlar as proof that the "slimy trail of Oriental moral degeneracy leads through the laundry to the gambling hall." He argued that, unless "the lid is put on and kept on in Chinatown," white men and women were at risk of being corrupted.[291] City police reacted immediately. The entire civic police force raided Wing Kee's laundry the evening after Pedlar's call to action appeared in print.

Both newspapers reported fulsomely on the raid, a new editor at the *District Ledger* treating it as a comic spectacle, Pedlar basking in the influence of the *Free Press*. Twenty men taking part in a game of fan tan were arrested and marched "in bunches" at gunpoint to the city jail, their queues tied together to prevent escape. How Foon promptly paid $1,000 in bail, and See Woo, a long-time Fernie resident, was subsequently charged with running a common gaming house.[292] Frustrated when the charge was dismissed at trial for lack of evidence that gambling was actually taking place, police soon engineered a sting operation—this time with a focus on drug use. A disgruntled Mah Chung, believing he had been cheated at Wing

THE DEPARTMENT OF THE INTERIOR.

CHINESE IMMIGRATION BRANCH.

No. **36169**

OCT 1 7 1919 191

To the Controller of Chinese Immigration,

Port of **VICTORIA, B. C.**

I hereby give notice that I desire to leave Canada with the intention of returning thereto. I propose to sail or depart from **VICTORIA, B. C.** for **HONG KONG,** on the **CANADA MARU** day of **OCT 1 7 1919** 191

I intend to return to Canada at the port of

I request registration and I attach my photograph hereto and give the following information for the purpose of my identification on my return.

My proper name is **Gee Foon**

I am sometimes known as

I first came to Canada in the year **1902**

My place of residence in Canada is **Fernie B C**

Where I have resided since the year **1902**

Certificate of Registration Form C. I. & No. **33 711**

My present occupation is that of **cook**

My place of birth was **Chong On**

My present age is **40**

Height **5** feet **6** inches.

Facial marks or other peculiarities

I am personally known to **Wong Wa** and **Lee Lui** both of **Victoria** to whom I would refer you for correctness of statements herein made.

朱寬

I have personally examined the person of Chinese origin who claims to be the person above described and whose photograph is affixed hereon (2), who returned to Canada on the day of **AUG 4 1920** 191 , and declare him to be the same person.

Dated at **VICTORIA, B. C.** Aug 4 1920 191

Long-time resident Gee Foon is found at Fernie in the census of 1911, but is not identified as a relative of How Foon. LAC, RG 76, Immigration Branch, Immigrants from China, 1889-1949

Kee's establishment, accepted a dollar from police to buy opium. This led to the arrest of How See for selling opium, another trial—with the county courtroom, according to the *Free Press*, "polluted with Chinks"—and an acquittal a few weeks later. Pedlar soon lamented it seemed impossible to secure a conviction for opium use under Canadian law.[293]

Although but a few Chinese residents could read English, most could readily understand the spoken language. Aware of the prejudice so frequently fostered against them by the local newspapers, their everyday experiences must also have sometimes revealed that prejudice. Yet they remained and they persevered. The *Henderson's Directory* of 1910 identifies seven laundries (Hop Kee, Hop Shing, How Hing, How Foon, Sam Lee, See Wo, Wing Kee), two restaurants (How Foon, Chew Chong) and a Chinese goods store run by Kim Tuck Wink Kee.[294] The directory listing is likely incomplete (indeed, How Foon's Chinese goods store is not included), but it provides a clear indication that Chinese-owned businesses were well established.

The 1911 census supports that conclusion. More than six dozen men comprised the Chinese bachelor community of Fernie, almost all of them employed as kitchen and laundry workers. Approximately half were living on Baker Avenue, but just as many are found in the several laundries and stores toward the northern end of Victoria Avenue. A small laundry was also located in the Annex on Mason Avenue and Chinese market gardens were operating south of the city limits. At Coal Creek, laundries were located at 304 and 307 Welsh Camp, and the boarding house again employed a Chinese cook as well as a laundryman.[295] Curiously, the census enumerator indicated that most Chinese had "no religion," while those living with How Foon were all identified as Anglican, and those at Coal Creek had apparently become Presbyterian.

Clearly, census data must be used with caution, yet the names— many of them illegible—and details found in the census for most of these men are all that remain of them in the historical record. Apart from the names of businesses identified in directories and newspapers, the same lack of information applies just as readily to entrepreneurs as it does to transient labourers. Not all small businesses are listed in directories. Even the most established owners of stores, laundries and restaurants, such as Sam Lee, Joe Sing and Wing Kee, all of whom were in business for many years, have left nothing apart from their names in local historical records. .

The exception to this observation was How Foon, Fernie's most prominent Chinese businessman. The store established at the corner of Cox and Baker in 1899 was almost certainly his. Advertisements for "China Goods" that began appearing in the *Free Press* ahead of Christmas 1903 identify him as the owner.[296] The *Henderson's Directory* of 1903 names him as the owner of a store and a laundry. Occasional newspaper items provide clear indications of his growing affluence and the continuing expansion of his business interests. In 1904, he was reported to have paid the very substantial sum of $675 in import duties.[297] By 1905, he is also identified as owner of the Fernie Restaurant. The two-storey How Foon block—constructed in 1909 to house the laundry, store, restaurant, accommodation for Foon and his workforce, and space for other businesses—was admired by the *District Ledger* as "one of the finest in the city," with the *Free Press* commenting during its construction that: "A Chinaman will have one of the most handsome blocks in the city."[298] By 1910, he was being described as "a wealthy Chinaman of the town."[299]

Although other Chinese businessmen may have had male relatives with them in Fernie, Foon is the only one for whom that can be confirmed from census data. Lee Bing Foon, who, as noted above, came to Fernie in 1898, was probably a relative, and How Hum Foon was a student at the public school in 1905.[300] When How Foon returned from a lengthy visit to China in 1908, he was accompanied by five new immigrants, one of whom was his son.[301] The census of 1911 identifies his three sons, a brother and four cousins amongst the nearly two dozen residents of the Foon property at Baker and Cox. Foon was also the only Chinese resident clearly reported to be an "employment agent."[302] Whether he acted in that capacity only for his own relatives and lodgers or in a broader capacity is not known. If, as seems likely, Foon paid the head tax for those who accompanied him to Fernie in 1908, they would have been obliged to repay him through their labour on his behalf.

Stanley left the *District Ledger* in 1910 to start his own printing business and the editors who succeeded him all brought a significant change in tone. John Bennett and then H.P. Nerwich still reported on matters involving Chinese residents as if they were comical events, but did not give voice to the racial animosity so clearly expressed by Stanley. When Frank Newnham took over in 1913, the humorous tone was also abandoned. The question of Chinese labour in the local mines—apparently settled—received barely a mention. Until the newspaper ceased publication in the summer of 1915, most references to Chinese residents were in connection with donations to community events and war-related fundraising.

Wah Ying Chong's store at the corner of Victoria Avenue and Rogers Street provides an incidental backdrop in an image symbolic of the faint Chinese footprint surviving in the region's historical record. Fernie & District Historical Society 5804do c.1921

At the *Free Press*, owner John Wallace apparently took over as editor in 1912, but there is no evident change in editorial policy or tone.[303] The newspaper in 1911 declared it would "prefer to see the Vancouver Chinese send themselves instead of Canadian dollars to fight the Manchu dynasty," and in 1913 still found much humour in customers refusing to pay their bills at local Chinese restaurants.

When the Chinese cook at a brothel suffered a serious head wound during an armed robbery, he was identified as "a stomach-destroyer in a kitchen in a southern suburb of the city" and named only as "Lee Something-or-other."[304]

However, the outbreak of the Great War coincided with a significant change in the reportage of the *Free Press* on matters pertaining to Chinese residents. Without the disparaging words of pre-war days, the newspaper included a few items of Chinese business and personal news, while most references were to prizes donated for events such as the annual curling bonspiel. Frequent contributions to the local Patriotic Fund and Red Cross collections by the Imperial Order Daughters of the Empire (IODE) were also noted. On one occasion in 1914, Chinese donors were specifically thanked by the IODE, who noted foreign-born participation in the fundraising effort was "a tribute to British laws and liberty."[305] In the community at large, there were also fewer indications of the pre-war prejudices. The Royal Hotel stopped advertising an all-white help policy in 1914. The Fernie Steam Laundry, after several changes in ownership, finally closed in 1916. In 1918, when representatives of the Federated Chinese Benevolent Association visited to exhume the bones of Chinese dead at Fernie, the *Free Press* described their efforts with evident respect.[306]

The end of the war saw the resumption of raids, with city police being assisted by members of the new Royal North-West Mounted Police detachment. Found guilty of importing opium, laundry owner Jim Lee was fined $300 by Police Magistrate Whimster, a penalty far greater than the $100 fines imposed on Jang Fang, Mah Wing and Joe Sing for possession of alcohol contrary to the provincial Prohibition Act.[307] Such raids and fines were reported by the *Free Press*, but without the tones of outrage that had been so evident in the pre-war years. Apart from the regular police raids and occasional donations to civic events, the Chinese presence in Fernie received practically no attention from Wallace at the *Free Press* in the post-war years. Even when the raising of prices at all laundries by a uniform 25 percent and a subsequent strike by laundry workers clearly suggested conflict between employers and employees, the matter was not explored.[308] The annual circus surrounding collection of the poll tax continued to be reported.[309]

Of course, without sensation, there is little to attract attention from newspaper editors. And there was nothing sensational about the well-established Chinese community, with merchants and a labour force attending to the same occupations as had their predecessors a quarter of a century earlier. The census of 1921 found essentially the same number of Chinese men living in Fernie as had the census of 1911. They were working in hotels, restaurants, laundries and in market gardening. The Fernie Club employed a Chinese steward, the RCMP barracks a Chinese chef and a few of Fernie's wealthier families had engaged Chinese domestics. The *Wrigley's British Columbia Directory* of 1921 identifies five laundries, three restaurants and five stores operating under Chinese ownership. Some of the merchants named a decade earlier are not found in Fernie in the immediate post-war years, but many familiar names remained. Laundry operators were How Foon, Hop Sing, Hung Hing, Jim Lee and Sam Lee. Stores offering dry goods and/or groceries were run by How Foon, Hong Sing, Wing Lee Yuen, Wah Ying Chong and Wing Hong Chong, restaurants by How Foon, Joe Sing and Wu Foy.[310] At his fine building on Baker Avenue, How Foon certainly remained the community's most prominent businessman, but fully two-thirds of Fernie's Chinese residents lived in the laundries and stores around the intersection of Victoria Avenue and Rogers Street, just past the Central School. Away from the core locations, a laundryman and a cook were found on Lindsay Avenue. A cook at the boarding house in Coal Creek was the only Chinese man enumerated there.

Fundamentally, it must be acknowledged that the experience of any individual or group of people can only be superficially accessed through newspapers and directories and census data. So many questions remain about the first quarter-century of Chinese residence in Fernie. Might there have been a room somewhere serving as a joss house? Was there an amateur photographer amongst them akin to Chow Dong Hoy of Quesnel or Yucho Chow of Vancouver? What were the attitudes of Chinese cooks, gardeners and laundrymen toward their employers, their customers and their neighbours? Would the many Chinese living in Hosmer, Michel, the Crowsnest Pass and Elko have preferred to be in Fernie? Despite the geographic isolation of the Elk Valley, did coal-based Fernie live up to expectations as Gold Mountain? Was Fernie unique in that no merchant was joined there by a wife and family?[311]

It must also be said that the beauty of a historical journey is also its danger: discoveries can dismay just as easily as they can delight.

Although Fernie did not witness atrocities such as those committed against the Chinese in the United States and was not the site of anti-Asian riots as was Vancouver, it is nevertheless clear that many in Fernie shared the attitudes that led to those calamities. The degree to which newspaper comment reflects opinion within a community can always be questioned, but it must do so at least to some extent. It is ironic that the most informative sources about Chinese life in Fernie were fundamentally hostile. Racist attitudes toward Chinese immigrants prevailed everywhere in British Columbia; there is no reason to believe Fernie could have been an exception. What truly dismays is that expressions of those attitudes in local newspapers a century ago are comparable with the worst excesses found on some social media platforms today.

POSTSCRIPT

Joe Sing is one of more than a dozen Chinese men interred at the Fernie Heritage Cemetery. The advertised "All White Help" policy of the Royal Hotel apparently did not apply to the hotel's restaurant in 1909 when Sing was assaulted there by two customers refusing to pay for their meal. The culprits were quickly arrested, but the *District Ledger* commented that they had made Sing "sorry he had ever left the land of flowers, sunshine and unlaundered shirts." Twice in 1913, as operator of the Depot Restaurant, Sing faced violence from customers refusing to pay for meals, the incidents receiving supposedly humorous reporting in the *Free Press*.[312] Sing was eighty-eight when he died in Fernie, a resident of Canada since 1883. He had not joined the general drift of Chinese men to Vancouver and Victoria in the years following the Chinese Exclusion Act of 1923. Joe Sing spent almost all his adult life in the Elk Valley, a member of the Chinese bachelor community of which barely a trace remains.

"Pretty Good Stuff"

Thomas Uphill and the Working Man's Beer

Thomas Uphill, the MLA for Fernie from 1921 to 1960, remains a unique figure in the history of British Columbia. First elected as a candidate for the Federated Labour Party in 1921, returned as a member of the Canadian Labour Party in 1924, and then sitting as an Independent Labour candidate for the next thirty years, Uphill holds the distinction of being the longest-serving MLA in the province's history. All major political parties—Conservative, Liberal, Social Credit and CCF—made concerted but unsuccessful efforts to unseat him. He worked consistently hard for his constituents in the Elk Valley and spoke forcefully on behalf of working people, the unemployed and the poor. One public stance that gained him much attention but little applause throughout his political career was his defence of what he regarded as the working man's fundamental right to enjoy a beer.

As mayor of Fernie during much of the Great War, and as the unsuccessful Conservative candidate in the provincial election of 1916, Uphill made no secret of his opposition to the prohibition of sales and consumption of alcohol. In the referendum that accompanied that election, the constituency of Fernie was one of only four in the province to vote against the proposed prohibition legislation; and, with almost 58 percent of those voting opposed, it was the riding that did so most convincingly.[313] However, arguments combining patriotism and the goal of social improvement carried the day across the province. After much delay and controversy surrounding the soldiers' vote from Europe, provincial prohibition of the sale of alcoholic beverages to residents of British Columbia came into effect on October 1, 1917.[314]

Despite their triumph, supporters of prohibition still had much to complain about. The manufacture of alcoholic beverages was not prohibited by the provincial legislation. Breweries could produce their beers for export to other provinces, and retailers could continue to sell wines and spirits to customers not living in British Columbia. With all provinces but Quebec dry by the end of 1917, prohibitionists called for the elimination of those loopholes. The federal government responded by banning the manufacture and interprovincial sale of liquor after March 1918. The only beer then legally available for sale or consumption in British Columbia was the watery brew of approximately 1.5 percent alcohol by volume that was popularly, but disdainfully, referred to as near-beer or 2-percent beer. Uphill insisted that such beverages were "a waste of good water."

Ironically, liquor of any strength was still available through a doctor's or druggist's prescription. This very wide loophole, and the well-stocked cellars of those who could afford to purchase booze before regulations took effect, meant that prohibition—whether or not it was so intended—had the effect of being class legislation. Uphill's working-class constituents typically had no such well-stocked cellar and little financial ability to purchase hard liquor by prescription for whatever its purpose might be. Hard liquor was not their preference, anyway. The popular belief that beer was the drink of the working-man was firmly grounded in reality. (Although women also worked in blue-collar jobs, particularly during the war years, they were not associated in the popular imagination with beer drinking, which was seen as a masculine pastime.)

Voters throughout the province became increasingly disgusted with the hypocrisy and loopholes that bedevilled the Prohibition Act. The spectacle of Prohibition Commissioner Walter Findlay being fined for bootlegging in 1918 and imprisoned for the same offence the following year only underlined the prevailing post-war opinion that prohibition had clearly failed to achieve any degree of social improvement. The second pillar of prohibitionist argument, patriotic support for the war effort, crumbled as the peace treaties were signed in Europe in 1919. Well aware that the question of liquor sales and consumption was highly divisive—particularly within both the governing Liberal Party and organized labour—the government decided to consult the electorate once more.

As Uphill was contemplating a second bid for the Fernie seat, the referendum of October 1920 asked simply if prohibition—under new regulations to close significant loopholes—should be continued or instead abandoned in favour of government control of the sale of alcoholic products. Prohibitionists believed that women—eligible to vote provincially for the first time—would help to ensure the continuation of "the dry option." When fully 62 percent of voters province-wide opted for government control, prohibitionists were quick to blame the result on "the immaturity" of female voters.[315] The *Fernie Free Press* welcomed the result by commenting that the "Prohibition Act had proved such a farce that to vote for its continuance seemed a joke."[316] Uphill saw the decision as a return to common sense and applauded his home constituency for voting nearly three to one against a continuation of prohibition. When a provincial election was called later that month, Uphill—who had recently lost his job as mayor of Fernie in a municipal election—announced he would make a second attempt to win provincial office.

As one of three successful Federated Labour Party candidates when the election results were announced in December 1920, Uphill thanked his working-class constituents for their support and declared that he would stand with them in the march "forward to victory over the class that has so long held us in subjugation."[317] Militant though this seems, Uphill was no revolutionary. He soon annoyed his more doctrinaire supporters by being the first Labour representative to attend the traditional dinner and dance for MLAs held at Government House. His maiden speech in the legislature was all about employment, unemployment and pensions for workers—themes to which he would return repeatedly over the course of his political career. But by far the greatest issue before the first session of the newly elected legislature was how to frame legislation to deal with the results of the referendum approving the government sale and distribution of alcohol. And it was on that contentious issue that Uphill came to the attention of the province at large.

The proposed government liquor bill specified that alcoholic beverages would be available in sealed packages to customers who had qualified to make purchases by paying an annual $5 fee. Veterans groups argued that beer should also be available in their clubs, and Uphill contended that workers' clubs should have the same privilege. Supporting the addition of a "beer clause" that would permit the sale of beer by the glass in such clubs, Uphill spoke eloquently in favour of "good beer and letting it run as free as possible." He declared: "When I mention beer I mean good draft beer and I would prosecute anyone who would brew this two percent stuff." He argued that beer should also be available in bars in remote locations, as "boys in these places are as entitled to some civilization as the boys living on the coast." Fundamental to his argument was his belief that beer made widely available would greatly curtail or even "eliminate the hard stuff," the consumption of which he insisted found no favour with him. As a Methodist, Uphill was well aware that most adherents of his church formed the bedrock of prohibitionist opinion in British Columbia. He shared their intolerance for drunkenness but consistently opposed all fresh initiatives to ban the consumption of hard liquor. Explaining that nuanced stance, he insisted that government cannot "make people good by legislation."[318]

There was considerable public support for including a beer clause in the new legislation, but it was soon obvious that its advocates were in a minority in the legislature. Even fellow Federated Labour MLA Samuel Guthrie opposed the beer clause, insisting that workers needed to remain clear-headed to focus on social and political realities. In committee, the proposal found only a dozen supporters, prompting Uphill to remark: "That's thirty-two for whisky and twelve for beer." He managed to introduce a beer clause of his own during third reading—proposing that "pretty good stuff" of roughly 4 percent alcohol by volume should be made available in clubs and at meetings of societies—but it, too, went down to defeat.[319] Instead, the new Liquor Control Board was authorized to sell beer only in sealed packages to customers who had paid an annual licence fee. With curtained windows and sparsely decorated interiors, government retail stores opened throughout the province in June 1921. Uphill undoubtedly would have been pleased that one of the initial suppliers of beer to these outlets was his hometown Fernie-Fort Steele Brewing Company.[320]

There were so many problems with the new system and so much avoidance of its regulations that yet another referendum accompanied the provincial election of June 1924. Voters were asked if they would approve of the sale of beer by the glass in licensed premises. A bare majority of voters said no, but the more remote districts that Uphill insisted were "entitled to some civilization" were heavily supportive. His own riding of Fernie voted four to one in favour. Predictably, Uphill's advocacy of easier access to beer drew the ire of prohibitionists. From his pulpit at Victoria City Temple, Pastor Clem Davies thundered that hundreds in "the bibulous community" of Fernie needed bread rather than beer, and he condemned Uphill for attempting to force "filthy poison down the throats" of British Columbians. The MLA for Fernie avoided comparably strong language in response but would eventually describe prohibitionists as "minority fanatics."

The newly elected provincial government agreed to let local results prevail. Victoria, for example, remained dry, while hotels in neighbouring Esquimalt—immediately to the west of

Thomas Uphill, MLA for Fernie, 1921-1960. Royal BC Museum and Archives B-06782

the provincial capital—and in far distant Fernie applied for beer licences. After further delay and confusion, the amended Liquor Act giving sanction to the new system was passed in December. This time twenty-eight out of the forty-eight MLAs voted for beer.

And so, in March 1925, the beer parlour was born. It did not offer the congenial social atmosphere of a British pub or a workingman's club such as Uphill had in mind, and he was quick to complain about the ridiculous attendant regulations. Beer was served one glass at a time to patrons who were forbidden to stand with drinks in hand. Food, cigarettes and non-alcoholic drinks were banned from premises that were just as joyless as the government liquor stores. There was considerable pressure to ban women, as well, to the point that women were effectively excluded, by custom if not by legislation, from entering the beer parlours that opened in 1925.[321] If Uphill expressed an opinion initially on that latter point, it went unreported. However, when challenged during one of the debates in the legislature if a working man's wife should enjoy a beer, he replied quickly, "She can have one, too."

The return of beer by the glass did not end the public debate over the availability of alcohol, but it did represent a limited victory for the position advocated by Uphill. The absurdities of the legislation and the sterile atmosphere of the beer parlours continued to attract his comment, but working men did once again find their beer accessible and affordable. In Fernie and the many other districts that had voted affirmatively in the referendum, that aspect of the battle had been won. When the Liquor Act was opened up for amendments in 1927, Uphill again pressed unsuccessfully for private clubs to have the same right as beer parlours to sell beer by the glass.[322] At the same time, working-class women—and their middle-class counterparts—won the right to enter beer parlours to enjoy a drink, but only through a separate entrance.

For the remainder of his political career, Uphill focused primarily upon mining legislation, unemployment insurance, pensions and working conditions. However, during the middle years of the Second World War—shortly after he had been re-elected for the fifth time—the forces that brought about prohibition in 1917 returned to strength. Arguments again emerged to insist that devoting grain production to the manufacture of alcohol was harmful to the war effort. Under Order-in-Council PC 11374, the federal government brought in regulations late in 1942 to restrict the manufacture and sale of beer and spirits nationwide. The fact that he was a provincial politician did not stop Uphill from bringing a strongly worded motion before the legislature in March 1943 urging MLAs to press Ottawa to repeal the restrictions on beer.

His return to the barricades gained him widespread condemnation in some quarters and much applause in others. Speaking to his motion, Uphill insisted, "Men working in hot conditions need a glass of beer and no one working in a white collar occupation has any right to deny them their beer." Brandishing a bottle of beer as he spoke, Uphill was accused by other MLAs of having consumed its contents on the floor of the legislature. Feigning outrage, he insisted that the bottle was empty when he brought it in. It was only to make a point, he said, and Uphill did indeed make clear what that point was when he summed up: "Beer is as necessary to the worker as milk is to the baby... Hands off the workers' beer." His fellow MLAs apparently did not like the "strong stuff" his motion represented. They passed a milder resolution asking the federal government simply to "give further consideration" to the restrictions on beer production.[323]

The federal government was not inclined to reconsider. Uphill continued to press for the reversal of wartime beer restrictions, urging workers angered by them not to withdraw their support for war bonds in protest. The "No Beer, No Bonds" campaign was an expression of opposition to the regulations and an attempt to apply pressure to have them reversed. The campaign failed to draw widespread support from any quarter, and it certainly did not draw Uphill's. Prohibition during the Great War had not dampened his enthusiastic efforts to promote the sale of Victory Bonds, and restrictions on beer production during the Second World War did nothing to weaken his endorsement of war bonds.[324] He was certainly pleased when, with the prospect of a federal election looming, the government cancelled the restrictions in March 1944.

Uphill was still an MLA when the City of Victoria finally ended more than thirty years of its local prohibition of beer sales by the glass in 1954. It is tempting to imagine the member for Fernie sneaking out a back door of the legislature to visit the beer parlours of Esquimalt during all those years, but imagination would lead far from the truth on this point. The irony is that the champion of the workingman's right to enjoy a beer was not a frequent patron of beer parlours. He would nevertheless have been aware that the concentration of ownership in the Canadian brewing industry was resulting in a decline in both the quality and variety of beers available during the 1950s. And he would certainly have been saddened to see his hometown brewery—no longer an independent but for some years functioning instead as part of Interior Breweries after merging with Kootenay Breweries of Nelson—close completely in 1959 when the company moved all production two hundred kilometres away to Creston.

According to newspaper reports, Uphill in 1959 was still vigorous in his espousal of causes he held dear and still able to entertain his fellow MLAs and the public gallery whenever he spoke on any topic in the legislature.[325] But with health becoming a concern, he decided not to run in the election of 1960. He died in 1962, the death certificate identifying his occupation as "MLA for Fernie (retired)." More than half a century later, today's working man and working woman and their middle-class counterparts no longer need a Thomas Uphill to lobby for reasonable access to beer. Restrictions on the availability of alcohol in bars, clubs and restaurants in British Columbia were progressively peeled away by successive governments; provincial liquor stores have long since removed the curtains from their windows. With the proliferation of independent craft breweries, the quality and variety of beers now available ensure that the "pretty good stuff" he so consistently fought for can readily be found in retail outlets and consumed in public settings far more conducive to enjoyment than the austere beer parlours introduced in the 1920s. In the long run, Uphill won those battles.

Postscript

Thomas Uphill's career has been forgotten by all but the most serious students of British Columbia's history.[326] Reported to be the longest-serving elected politician in what was then the British Empire, he was chosen as the first MLA to greet Princess Elizabeth when she visited the legislature in 1951.[327] He is perhaps most remembered for his initial support of Social Credit Party leader W.A.C. Bennett—support he quickly regretted—which allowed that party to take power in British Columbia in 1952. Perhaps because no major political party spoke on his behalf when awards were being considered, or perhaps because he was so often the defender of unpopular positions, Uphill is not remembered by a memorial anywhere in the province. The legislature in Victoria contains no plaque to draw attention to its longest-serving MLA; the city of Fernie made him a freeman in 1956 but has not otherwise commemorated his career. A seniors housing facility—the result of a community initiative in 1958 to mark the province's centennial year—opened in Fernie in 1962 and stands alone in recalling his name.

But recently, impressed by Uphill's consistent advocacy for the right of working people to enjoy their hard-earned beer, Swan's Brewpub in Victoria decided that an appropriate way to recall that stance would be to name a suitable beverage in his honour: Tommy Uphill IPA, maybe; or perhaps Thomas Uphill ESB—the Working

Man's Beer. In 2018, the brewer settled upon Thomas Uphill Amber Ale as the kind of beverage that would have appealed to workers a century ago. An official beer launch attracted historians, politicians and Uphill's descendants. The ale appealed to modern tastes and remained in production for three years. Whatever your preferred brew, beer drinkers of British Columbia, unite! Raise a glass in memory of Thomas Uphill.

THREE GLIMPSES OF GINGER

WHEN ALBERT GOODWIN
CAME TO TOWN

lbert "Ginger" Goodwin remains a shadowy figure. Despite serious attention from historians, only a broad outline of his career has emerged, and virtually nothing is known of his private life. His few published writings and his political activities reveal much about his philosophy, but leave the unavoidable impression of a one-dimensional figure. Still clouded by controversy and uncertainty are the circumstances surrounding his refusal to report for military service and the violent death he met as a consequence of that refusal. Perhaps a look at the time he spent in the Crowsnest Pass/Elk Valley region—as an avid footballer, a determined political agent and a driver in a coal mine—could help bring the man just a small step or two further into focus.

THE LEATHER CHASER

Albert Goodwin arrived in the Crowsnest Pass in April 1910. Given the boom conditions of the day, he probably would have been able to find work at any mining camp in the region. Passing through the Alberta mining communities of Lethbridge, Passburg, Hillcrest, Coleman and Bellevue, he and two friends from the coal mines of Nova Scotia got off the train—by chance or design is not known—at Michel in British Columbia. Close to the border with Alberta, the mines at Michel were owned and operated by the Crow's Nest Pass Coal Company. Like most communities with the sole purpose of mining coal at the time, Michel was enjoying prosperous times. The population had increased to approximately two thousand people, but it was not a pretty place. Nor was it a particularly safe place. In April 1910, residents were pressing for improvements to basic amenities, with sanitation being the greatest concern.

Branch 16 of the Socialist Party of Canada (SPC) was active at Michel and held regular meetings on Sunday afternoons. Those meetings may have been Goodwin's first exposure to politics in British Columbia, but there is nothing in surviving documents to indicate how he spent his Sundays. What is known is what he did on Saturdays. If Sunday was for church and politics, Saturday was for football, and the game was exceptionally popular amongst the miners. Goodwin and his companions quickly won places on the team representing Michel Football Club in the Crow's Nest Pass Football League. There were two prizes to be had: the league championship and the Mutz Cup—named after its donor, Albert Mutz of the Fernie-Fort Steele Brewing Company. The season started well for Michel, with three successive league victories. Goodwin proved to teammates and spectators alike that he was an exceptional player. His ability as a goal scorer was noted in local newspaper reports, on one occasion at least drawing high praise.[328]

Over the course of the season, Michel played home and away league matches with Bellevue, Coal Creek, Coleman, Fernie, Frank, and Hosmer, and travelled to Cranbrook and Moyie for cup ties. Michel won the league championship, but was eliminated early from play for the Mutz Cup. Just as league play was finishing in late September, the mines at Michel went on short time. That meant miners spent more time out in the community and at their boarding houses. Coincidentally, the provincial medical health officer visited Michel on September 17. He condemned the lack of even rudimentary provision for sanitation and reported that "odours exist around the houses of a most offensive character."[329] It is tempting to consider that the conjunction of these circumstances may have changed the course of history in British Columbia. With the team's season apparently over and with reduced opportunities for work, Goodwin and his Nova Scotian cohorts left Michel in early October with hopes of finding employment in the mines at Cumberland on Vancouver Island.[330]

THE POLITICAL ACTIVIST

Three and a half years later, in March 1914—during dramatically different circumstances for himself, for the coal industry and for the political philosophy he had embraced—Goodwin again came to East

Albert "Ginger" Goodwin. Cumberland Museum and Archives C110-002

Kootenay. In Cumberland, he had become active with the Socialist Party of Canada, but these were discouraging times for socialists. In Alberta, the SPC's only MLA was defeated in 1913 in a riding that included the mining communities of the Crowsnest Pass. In British Columbia, the socialist share of the popular vote declined in the election of 1912. Only two socialist MLAs had been elected—both from the mining districts of Nanaimo—and they were being ignored by the overwhelming Conservative majority in the legislature.

However, in the Elk Valley and the Crowsnest Pass, something was afoot for the SPC. In early February, the *District Ledger* newspaper noted: "It is hoped within the course of the next few weeks to have stationed in the Pass one of the best-posted Socialists from the Coast, who will take up the quest of a permanent organizer and systematically organize the whole of the district."[331] The individual was not named. At the same time, but without comparable advance publicity, Alf Budden—the best-posted socialist lecturer in Alberta—was also preparing for a speaking tour of the district.[332] Clearly, SPC organizations in both British Columbia and Alberta were paying close and particular attention to the coal-mining region that straddled the southernmost border between the two provinces. The reason for that attention was a political initiative being proposed by the miners' union.

That initiative was an item on the agenda of the upcoming annual convention of District 18 of the United Mine Workers of America (UMWA). Stretching from Fernie through the Crowsnest Pass of Alberta to beyond Lethbridge, and with at least six thousand members,

District 18 was the largest union in western Canada at the time. Delegates to the convention, scheduled for mid-February in Lethbridge, were preparing to consider a motion submitted by the Michel local union declaring socialism the official political philosophy of the organization. Going one step further, the local union representing miners at Fernie and Coal Creek proposed adding a clause to the District 18 constitution that read: "We pledge ourselves to political action as laid down by the Socialist Party of Canada."

In Fernie, Branch 17 of the Socialist Party seemed particularly vigorous. Most of its membership was drawn from the Fernie/Coal Creek local union of the UMWA. In February, at the same time the announcement was made about the expected arrival of a permanent organizer for District 18, the branch decided its storefront room in the Miners' Union Building on Victoria Avenue was not large enough for an expanded program of regular debates and social activities. A building on Pellatt Avenue had recently become available when a businessman running a roller rink wrapped up his operation. When the socialist clause at the District 18 convention—after prolonged debate—was adopted as anticipated, Branch 17 immediately took out a lease on the former roller rink. The *District Ledger*—the newspaper owned and operated by District 18—noted that the lease would indeed be an ambitious undertaking, but shared the optimism of local SPC members that they would be able to meet the financial obligations required to move into "one of the most commodious halls of the city."[333]

And it is at this point—just ten days after District 18 aligned with the Socialist Party of Canada, and while the Fernie branch of that party made preparations to move into its new home—that Goodwin is first identified by name as the expected organizer from the coast. The *District Ledger* reported on February 28 that Albert Goodwin would arrive on March 8, noting that "Comrade Goodwin has had considerable experience speaking and organizing at the Coast, and has a most fluent knowledge of sociology."[334] The *District Ledger* consistently used the term sociology to refer to the economic critique of society developed by philosophers such as Karl Marx. And so the groundwork was laid for the arrival of Albert Goodwin: lecturer, sociologist, activist.

Expectations evidently were high and Goodwin wasted no time getting down to work. He arrived a week earlier than announced and went straight to Michel, his first stop on a lightning tour of Crowsnest mining camps. On the evening of March 1, he gave what was described as "a very powerful address to a good audience" in the Workers' Hall. [335] Crossing into Alberta, Goodwin was next "a hit with the miners of Bellevue," as he urged them to devote time to a study of their position in society so they could, as he said, be armed and prepared for the future. The local correspondent from Bellevue for the *District Ledger* concluded: "It would be a wise move on the part of the S. P. of C. if it is possible to have a permanent organizer of the calibre of Comrade Goodwin in District 18."[336]

The day after his speech in Bellevue, he travelled to Passburg looking for work.[337] As an emissary for the Socialist Party, Goodwin was likely not receiving a salary. He had to rely largely on the kindness of friends—both personal and ideological—for room, board and expenses. Such kindness has its limits. In order to remain in the Crowsnest, Goodwin needed to support himself. It is likely he explored the possibility of employment at every stop on his tour. However, at every stop, he was unsuccessful. Mines throughout the region had a surplus of workers in the spring of 1914; none of the mining companies was hiring.

After just one week in the Alberta Crowsnest, Goodwin wrote a letter to the *District Ledger*, ostensibly outlining the conclusions he had reached during his "trip through the Pass." He referred approvingly to the alignment of District 18 with the SPC, but noted he "could find no traces of organization so far as the Socialist Party of Canada is concerned." Instead of jumping to conclusions based on his short time in the region, Goodwin was actually identifying the reason the SPC and District 18 were eager to place an organizer in the Alberta Crowsnest. Despite so recently having had an SPC MLA, and despite the endorsement of the SPC by delegates at the recent District 18 convention, there was indeed no trace of SPC organization east of the provincial border. Goodwin knew that before he arrived. He also knew it was his mission to establish such organization, and urged his readers to correct the situation by establishing "a strong chain of locals" throughout the Pass. He urged his readers not to "neglect that which is in your vital interest, for the chains of wage slavery which bind and chafe will hold you down in the depths of slavery and humiliation so long as you are content to submit." He ends with the standard closing in letters written by members of the Socialist Party of Canada: "Yours in revolt, A. Goodwin, Organizer, S. P. of C."[338]

As a description of the problem he has to address and an assessment of its solution, the letter is perfectly clear. Unfortunately, the letter is the only surviving statement of Goodwin's thinking as he set about his task. Subsequent references in the *District Ledger* about Goodwin's speaking engagements are few. However, they do clearly indicate his efforts were wide-ranging. On the evening of Friday, March 27, he addressed miners in Taber, fifty kilometres east of Lethbridge. On the eastern edge of District 18 and certainly not in the Crowsnest, Taber was seldom on the itineraries of speakers and entertainment troupes. The fact that Goodwin went as far as Taber suggests he visited all the communities that were then home to local unions of District 18 in southern Alberta. He may or may not have been able to deliver speeches at each visit—and, curiously, there is no report of a speaking engagement in Lethbridge—but, as his letter indicates, he certainly would have been encouraging "people who understand the situation" in each community to advance the work of the SPC.

Goodwin was soon back in the Crowsnest Pass, speaking on April 3 at the Union Hall in Hillcrest. When the indoor meeting wrapped up, Goodwin got up on a soapbox in front of one of the hotels to speak further on the topic of "Political Economy." The open-air meeting was a favoured tactic of the SPC, and his soapbox speech at Hillcrest was likely not the only one he delivered. Following the visit, and indicating Goodwin's efforts were having an effect, intentions were announced to hold socialist meetings every Sunday evening in Hillcrest at the Union Hall.[339]

Two weeks later, not having found the employment that would have allowed him to remain and to act for the Socialist Party in the Alberta Crowsnest, Goodwin crossed back into British Columbia. It was an indication that his organizing efforts were coming to an end. He must have been hopeful that his work would result in specific support for the SPC, but he also would have known that, without employment, he could not remain in the region as a permanent organizer. He addressed the Michel local union on Sunday, April 19, the reporter stating only that the meeting "appreciated the able manner in which he handled his subject."[340]

The Michel Football Club held its fundraising dinner and dance the next day, Easter Monday. Was Goodwin in attendance?

It is interesting to note that, as he travelled throughout the region in March, the Crowsnest Pass Football League was in the process of organizing for the season. Meetings were being held in each participating community as questions about team finances and rosters were addressed. It must have been quite a mix of emotions for Goodwin: nostalgia, memory, perhaps aspiration to return to the playing field, and the knowledge he was competing philosophically for the attention of the game's players and spectators. In April, before league play got underway, friendlies were played every Saturday; it is likely he was a spectator on at least one occasion.

From Michel, it was south to Hosmer, where the CPR mines in the region were located and where he held a meeting in the dining room of the Queen's Hotel. On the evening of April 26, he spoke on "The Social Problem and its Solution" at the Socialist Hall in Fernie. The *District Ledger* reported the speech was well received and quoted Goodwin directly:

> The trade union movement all over the American continent has signally failed to wrest more of the products of their toil from the employing class, and has consequently outlived its usefulness in this respect… [T]he only solution is the one advocated by the Socialist party, and that is the overthrow of capitalism.

Goodwin had arrived in the region to bolster the connection between District 18 and the SPC, but, as his speech in Fernie indicates, the encouraging tone of his letter of early March had been replaced by an implicit criticism of his hosts. He must have known his efforts had been only minimally successful; he cannot have known even those small advances would be swept away in the tide of patriotism that followed the outbreak of hostilities in Europe just six months later. With a statement undermining the connection between his trade union hosts and the SPC, it is perhaps not surprising there was no invitation extended to speak at the grand May Day events scheduled to be held in Fernie one week later. The "permanent" organizer had lasted just eight weeks. Goodwin boarded the westbound CPR train on the morning of April 27, heading first to Kimberley and then to Nelson. In the columns of the *District Ledger*, the union newspaper which in February had so eagerly anticipated his arrival, his departure was barely noted.[341]

THE COAL MINER

Goodwin's third and final sojourn in the region began just before Christmas 1915. And once more, both personal and economic circumstances had changed dramatically. The bitter Vancouver Island coal strike had been over for a year, but Goodwin was not back at work in Cumberland. For his activism, he was one of those backlisted and banned from employment on the Island. That may explain his seeking employment again with the Crow's Nest Pass Coal Company, which was experiencing both a sharp increase in orders and a severe labour shortage. Partly due to remarkably high enlistment rates amongst coal miners for the battlefields of Europe, the labour shortage was also due to the internment of more than three hundred Austro-Hungarian and German nationals at Fernie six months earlier.

Under the guise of patriotism, in June miners at Coal Creek refused to work alongside German and Austro-Hungarian employees of the coal company. After union leaders refused to endorse their position, the rank and file membership went on strike; the provincial government donned the same patriotic mantle and ordered the immediate internment of so-called "enemy alien" employees of the Crow's Nest Pass Coal Company. Whatever else the internment crisis may have signified, it was a clear defeat for the socialist leadership of District 18. Goodwin had returned to a region where support for socialism was considerably weaker than it had been during his last visit less than two years earlier.[342]

Goodwin was hired by the Crow's Nest Pass Coal Company to work as a driver at the No. 1 East mine at Coal Creek. The company may have known of his being blacklisted on Vancouver Island; it may not have known. If Goodwin was happy to have found full employment in his area of expertise, he cannot have been too happy that so little work was available. Bitterly cold temperatures, high winds and exceptional snowfalls in January 1916 made outside activity all but impossible. The hospital was overwhelmed in treating cases of frostbite, and snowfalls and snow slides at Coal Creek caused further complications for mining operations.

The mines returned to full production at the end of the month, but February brought a new challenge to those with an interest in union politics. The inclusion in the District 18 constitution of the clause endorsing the Socialist Party of Canada remained controversial. The International UMWA, headquartered in Indianapolis, had been appalled by its adoption in 1914, and had tried unsuccessfully in 1915 to have it removed. Another attempt was on the agenda for the District 18 annual convention to be held in Fernie at the end of February.

Goodwin was invited to address the delegates on that issue, and—like so much pertaining to him—the speech he delivered generated controversy. The *District Ledger* newspaper was no longer publishing, so no detailed description of convention proceedings is available. In an interview many years later, one of the delegates in attendance remembered that Goodwin certainly spoke forcefully on that occasion. The *Fernie Free Press* reported that, following a rigorous debate, the convention agreed to remove the clause from the District 18 constitution. The fiercely anti-socialist editor of the *Free Press* took delight in the decision, and noted delegates refused to give Goodwin the usual vote of thanks for his address.[343] After a century and with so little reliable evidence to examine, all that remains is speculation about what Goodwin said and how he said it. He may well have returned to his topic of April 1914—noting the failure of trade unionism to make significant gains for the worker—and likely chided delegates for even considering the removal of the socialist clause from the constitution.

Many questions arise, but at this point fact must give way to more speculation. Was it simply a coincidence that Goodwin was working at Coal Creek when the convention addressed the constitutional question? It was well known the issue would be revisited. It might also be asked why Goodwin should be the Socialist Party member chosen to address the delegates. There were, after all, several residents of Fernie who, as members of both District 18 and the SPC, could have been invited to make the case for retention of the clause. Or is it reasonable to assume Goodwin had found work at Coal Creek specifically to advance and defend the interests of the Socialist Party, just as he hoped to do throughout the Crowsnest Pass in 1914? He may have been the intended speaker even before he arrived in Fernie.

Following the decision to end the affiliation of District 18 with the SPC, Goodwin quit work almost immediately. A letter dated March 6 written by Goodwin to Premier William Bowser concerning an interned miner from Cumberland is the last definite date we have for him in the region. He would never work again as a coal miner. In the historical record, he next appears at Trail in mid-May, participating in a meeting to reorganize the branch of the Socialist Party of Canada there.[344]

Goodwin seems a restless man, never staying long before leaving for other horizons. Apart from his participation in the Michel Football Club, very little information about his private life has emerged. Based on the letter to the *District Ledger*, his assignment in the Crowsnest in 1914 and his presentation to the District 18 convention in 1916, Goodwin's political outlook is certainly clear. It is also consistent with what is known about his actions and published writings elsewhere. Nevertheless, after fading in and out of focus in the fleeting glimpses of him in the Crowsnest Pass and the Elk Valley, Albert "Ginger" Goodwin leaves the region with many questions unanswered, still the well-known historical figure… even while so little is actually known about him.

Postscript

If the surviving impressions of Ginger Goodwin in the Elk Valley and Crowsnest Pass must remain vague, they stand in sharp relief at Cumberland, where he is remembered today as a working-class hero. Refusing to comply with an order to report for military service, he was shot and killed near Cumberland in July 1918. Almost everyone in town took part in his funeral procession, which was re-enacted on its centenary. A section of the Inland Island Highway nearby has been designated Ginger Goodwin Way by the provincial government.

Red Lights in Fernie

Remembering Lena Bell

The great fire of August 1908 is one of the defining events in the history of Fernie. For decades to follow, residents would talk of a day that seared itself into their individual and collective memories. After more than a century, the event and its aftermath deserve serious reassessment, but one fact remains certain: the death toll was remarkably low. One of those killed was described in all the newspaper reports only as a "woman from the restricted district." Lena Bell thereby became a footnote prudently glossed over in what quickly emerged as the narrative of a determined community rebuilding in triumph over devastation and despair. Yet when that footnote is given some consideration, it reveals a great deal about the social realities then current in Fernie. Whatever the attitude of the broader community toward her may have been, Lena Bell has something to say about local history.

During the last two years of the nineteenth century, the instant town of Fernie grew quickly to serve the interests of the Crow's Nest Pass Coal Company. Attracting professional men, entrepreneurs and, of course, workers to extract the "black gold" found in such abundance at nearby Coal Creek, the town also attracted con artists, carpetbaggers, whisky sellers and brothel keepers. More respectable residents were soon complaining. In March 1899, the *Fernie Free Press*—itself then just a year old—editorialized about "Bacchus Rampant" and urged local authorities to deal with the community's numerous illicit whisky stills and brothels.[345] It was the start of a search for respectability that would last two decades before achieving apparent success.

Newspaper owner George Henderson gave recurrent voice to concerns about morality and his campaign soon brought results. The number of liquor sellers began to decline, and, in May 1899, police conducted their first raid on the brothels. The *Free Press* provided full, front-page coverage. The magistrate fined the seventeen women brought before him (and another half-dozen in their absence) a total of $300. Frankie Scouten, one of six brothel keepers each fined $20, asked the magistrate how often she could expect to have to pay that amount. She was told that, unless she changed her ways, the next time could be the next day, next week or next month. The fine, the magistrate said, was not a fee for a licence.[346] Frankie Smith, who had been in Fernie just a few weeks, was soon faced with a charge for which the penalty was much clearer. In June, she was sentenced to two months in jail for assaulting another prostitute.[347]

Henderson continued his campaign against those he variously described as "gaily dressed courtesans," "nymphs of the pave" and "soiled doves." Complaining that a second raid in August had gathered and fined only half the town's "feathered beauties," he insisted respectable wives and daughters should be protected from the sight and even the knowledge of the vice. In an editorial, he wrote:

> [W]omen of ill-fame who flaunt their brazen faces and their gaudy finery in our streets, in our stores, and in some of our hotels, on weekdays and on Sundays, at all hours of the day and night should either be compelled to keep within doors or be driven from the town.

Insisting that respectable women should not have to shop alongside prostitutes, he concluded, "If the dragon is permitted to lurk in our midst it should at least be compelled to hide its head."[348]

After another raid in response to a citizen complaint a year later, police magistrate Herbert Trites fined five women as brothel keepers, amongst them Lilly "Whiskey Lil" McDonald and Mollie Rosencrantz, who were in business in two large houses opposite his residence.[349] (That must have resulted in an interesting neighbourhood dynamic.) Henderson continued to condemn "the notorious" Frankie Scouten and "the old hag" Rosencrantz. At Christmas time in 1900, police issued orders that brothel keepers and their boarders would be permitted on the streets only between four and six p.m., Monday, Thursday and Saturday. At least partially, Henderson had achieved his demand that the dragon should hide its head, although he wrote in disgust, "Might as well license and be done."

Frankie Scouten—a dressmaker according to the census return

of 1901—resided in one of the several brothels found in the old town area, but initially there was no single restricted district in Fernie. McDonald and Rosencrantz were in business at the extreme south end of Pellatt Avenue, and three smaller brothels were located in the sections of town not yet surveyed north of Cox Street. Race typically loomed large in reportage of the day and in his comments on the residents of these brothels, Henderson always mentioned if the individual "had some black blood in her veins," or was "decidedly dark in colour." On one occasion, he referred to the prostitutes of old town as "black spots on the face of the earth."[350]

Practically nothing is known of the women identified in newspaper reports, but because of information required by the Canadian census of April 1901, the racial identities and countries of origin of those enumerated are clear. Henderson's observations are confirmed by the census. Of the fifteen women then living in what were commonly called Fernie's "sporting houses," seven were White, five Black, and three were Japanese. Most came from the United States and only one was Canadian. Lena Bell is identified as a resident in a brothel north of Cox Street. She was one of the eleven Americans and one of five stated by the census to be Black. They were residents of a rough community on the resource frontier, and, if the example of Lena Bell is typical, they were not to be trifled with. When a miner refused to repay a modest loan he received from her, she quickly hired a local solicitor and won a judgment against him in civil court.[351]

In the early summer of 1901, police issued fresh orders that brothels had just thirty days to move outside the town limits. Frankie Scouten had already left for Michel, and enforcement of the new order may have persuaded the two brothels at the south end of Pellatt Avenue to close. No further reference is found in the *Free Press* to Whiskey Lil McDonald, and, in ill health, Mollie Rosencrantz moved to Seattle. A new owner/editor at the newspaper soon noted the death of "Old Mol" by dancing on her grave, advising readers she had recently moved to hell.[352] The brothels in the north end—located on either side of the rail line and reasonably close to the CPR depot—were already outside what were then the town limits. Unaffected by the police order, they became Fernie's restricted district.

The police orders to keep prostitutes off the streets except during specified times were enforced inconsistently, and, by the end of 1902, the *Free Press* complained "the vice" was apparent again at all hours

THE OLD TOWN AND "ROW."

3. The Crows Nest Pass Coal Company will use its influence to prevent any of the houses in the Old Town, or district back of the coke ovens or east of the lands of the Canadian Pacific railway from being used for hotels or other commercial purposes, and the Crows Nest Pass Coal Company agrees to cancel within six months from the date of incorporation all leases in the "Red Light District" and to dispossess the tenants, and also to set apart in the new municipality, lands which may be purchased by the said ejected tenants, to which they may remove their present tenements

Article 3 of the agreement between the Crow's Nest Pass Coal Company and the Fernie Board of Trade. *Fernie Free Press*, May 13, 1904.

of the day. Prostitutes interested in seeking entertainment and/or advertising themselves were taking prominent seats at concerts and public meetings. In November 1903, they were forbidden by the local chief of provincial police to attend such gatherings until provision could be made "for their special accommodation." It is doubtful such arrangements were ever provided, but it is clear that questions surrounding prostitution were of significant concern as the community of Fernie moved toward incorporation in 1904. The *Free Press* asserted that one of the strongest arguments in favour of incorporation was the ability to create a civic police force to deal with the "scores of evils" provincial police were powerless to address. The newspaper urged the new mayor and council to represent respectability in dealing with all the "tin-horn gamblers, pimps and prostitutes in Fernie."[353] At *The Ledge*, the community's new second newspaper, editor Robert Lowery called for a "happy medium," noting: "Any community absolutely under the power of church or saloon becomes unfit for the abode of free and intelligent human beings."[354]

When negotiations between the board of trade and the Crow's Nest Pass Coal Company were finally concluded, the coal company agreed to prohibit brothels on remaining company lands and to cancel the leases of all such establishments on land about to be transferred to an incorporated Fernie. However, ejected tenants would be allowed to purchase lots in Blocks 41 and 42, to which sites they could "remove their present tenements." Thus was created, "at the extreme limits of the townsite," the north end restricted district, bordered by Macpherson Avenue, Davies Street and Pellatt Avenue, and sanctioned by the City of Fernie.[355] By December, brothels were being moved onto purchased lots.

The establishment of an official restricted district had its critics, but it was an arrangement that resulted in income for the newly minted City of Fernie. At police court in September 1903, Lena Bell had been fined the modest sum of $5 for "keeping a disorderly house." It was one of the last such fines destined for provincial coffers. In April 1905, for "keeping a house of ill-fame," Marie Brown was fined $50 by city police—an amount surprisingly high, perhaps to express civic displeasure that she had recently moved from Cranbrook to establish herself in Fernie's new restricted district. Or perhaps the excessive penalty was imposed simply to raise needed funds. The finances of new City of Fernie were precarious. On one occasion in 1905, there were insufficient funds to pay the teachers' salaries due at the end of the month. A raid on the restricted district was authorized, fines were paid, and as the city clerk passed cheques to the principal, he remarked on "tainted money."[356] More moderate fines for others soon followed as the young city apparently settled on a standard $20 fine for offenders from the brothels.[357] An understanding amongst the city government, city police and the residents of the restricted district had been reached.

Moments of crisis were frequent. At Michel, where prostitutes from Fernie often visited, two of the community's three brothels were destroyed by separate fires in the summer of 1906. A Japanese man, identified in newspaper reports as "a procurer" from Chicago, broke into "Rosa's house" in Fernie to attack her and another woman— said to be unwilling to be procured—before making his escape. Both women were seriously wounded by him.[358] Although infrequent, veiled references in the *Free Press* suggest visiting pimps were typically recognized as unwelcome and potentially dangerous. When Frankie Smith brought charges of theft against a male associate, reportage of the trial revelled in the colourful details of the Black madam's appearance (and hinted at a rivalry with Lena Bell), but also made clear the potential for violence represented by the defendant.[359]

At the same time, local advocates of moral reform were beginning to organize. A branch of the Women's Christian Temperance Union (WCTU) was established at Fernie in the summer of 1906. Across the province, demands for the prohibition of gambling, alcohol and brothels were gathering strength. In May 1908, under the auspices of the WCTU, Ada Murcutt spent a week in Fernie lecturing each evening on topics ranging from votes for women, the evils of the liquor trade and the sophistication of Asian societies. Murcutt was an effective and entertaining advocate for causes of moral improvement, highly regarded at the coast and feted in Fernie by Mayor William Tuttle and the community's Protestant ministers. At the provincial conference of the WCTU in Victoria a month later, she said a mayor and a minister of religion in an Interior town had agreed there were not a dozen "pure girls" over the age of fifteen in their community. When she soon identified that community as Fernie, publicity across the province brought much unwelcome scrutiny and a firm denial from Mayor Tuttle that he had made such a statement.[360]

The scandal would likely have developed further had it not been entirely eclipsed by the great Fernie fire, which rapidly destroyed most of the city on the first day of August 1908. Lena Bell knew very well her occupation was fraught with perils, but she cannot have imagined she would meet her death by fire. One newspaper report mentions Bell was home with an illness at the time, but provides no hint about why she was physically unable to flee the advancing flames, or why two other resident prostitutes (who were initially thought also to have perished) could not help her to do so. Her death certificate states only that she was "burned to death in the fire at Fernie in her house on Pellatt Avenue." [361]

Like everything in the path of the fire, the restricted district was entirely destroyed. As the process of reconstruction progressed, for a few months Fernie lacked a restricted district. When it, too, rose from the ashes, the north end of Howland Avenue was not to be its location. The Free Press noted: "It seems to be recognized that the prostitutes are a necessary evil in this community and that a place must be found for them."[362] Civic authorities suggested a location near the river at the north end of the Annex, which was then outside city limits. Accordingly, a property there was sold to known prostitutes in October, but protests were soon heard. The District Ledger condemned "the vultures" who had sold the property and called for the removal of "the degenerates" who had purchased it.[363] A considerable debate took place about where and whether a restricted district sanctioned by the city should be established. The Ledger soon boasted of the success of its campaign to remove "these vipers from

An unidentified woman on Victoria Avenue, August 1908. Royal BC Museum and Archives b-06531-141

the Annex." It was soon reported that "brown pearls" were also being evicted from city hotels.[364]

It was a situation that both brothel keepers and civic politicians had to address. City council received a petition from brothel keeper Pearl Brown and others requesting that a property on Cokato Road be designated a restricted district, but asked the attorney general to grant city police jurisdiction over a separate property that council preferred. Significantly, both were located outside city limits. An arrangement such as the one authorizing the former Howland Avenue restricted district was not part of the discussion. By the end of November, amidst much uncertainty about how to proceed, decisions had been made. Standing for re-election, Mayor Tuttle said of the prostitutes, "If you try to do away with them entirely you will have them as your next door neighbour. Is it not better to keep them as far as possible from the city and under police surveillance?" According to the Methodist minister, W. Lashley Hall, Tuttle claimed to have refused a bribe to locate the restricted district on one proposed site and to have personally "paid the cheque for another."[365] While it remains unclear precisely what was meant by that, Tuttle certainly played a role in determining that the property requested by Pearl Brown—on Cokato Road just south of the brewery—received approval from the City of Fernie. Responsibility for policing the new restricted district was granted to the city by the attorney general. The provincial police were soon evicting any prostitutes still living in the Annex or anywhere else other than the approved location.[366]

The arrangement was not without its critics, and questions of public morality were central issues during the civic election of 1909. At the last moment,

W. W. TUTTLE.

Fernie Mayor William Tuttle. Royal BC Museum and Archives b06590-141

Tuttle decided not to seek re-election. The Fernie Trades and Labour Council created the Citizens' League, which declared itself for "a decent City, and the enforcement of all laws." Their mayoralty candidate, Louis Eckstein, stated he was "opposed to the system of opening the door to lawbreakers and licensing them." An aldermanic hopeful, William Dicken called for the abolition of gambling, closing saloons and pool rooms on Sunday, and "regulating the appearance of the restricted element in our streets and stores." He declared the "time has come to rid ourselves of their presence... I want only the support of the decent and respectable part of the electors—others I do not want."[367] He got the support he asked for, but no more. Dicken and the other aldermanic candidates endorsed by the Citizens' League finished at the bottom of the poll. Eckstein was also decisively defeated. Matters other than respectability proved of more concern to voters as merchants and professional men easily retained control of civic affairs. The election results effectively endorsed the arrangement made between brothel operators and city council.

Precisely what that arrangement meant financially for both prostitutes and the city is perfectly clear. Original police ledgers were destroyed in the fire, but records dating from 1909 indicate that the random raids and varying fines of the pre-incorporation days had long been replaced by what was essentially a system of monthly civic licensing. The spectacle of a police raid was no longer necessary as the women were summonsed to appear before the police magistrate on or near the last day of each month, when each "keeper of a house of ill fame" was fined $20 and each "inmate" $10. In April 1909, for example, those amounts were paid by seven brothel operators (Frankie Smith and Pearl Brown amongst them) and fourteen prostitutes. For that month and every month over the years that followed, no one so fined ever served the alternate penalty of up to a month in the city jail. Of the $4,518.50 collected in fines by the City of Fernie for the calendar year 1910, more than half came from the brothels of Cokato Road.[368]

However, opposition to that arrangement remained strong and soon found allies outside the local community. A tour of the western provinces by Presbyterian minister Dr. J.G. Shearer in November 1910 ignited firestorms on questions of morality in Winnipeg and Vancouver and resulted in a coordinated campaign by Fernie's Presbyterians and Methodists. A petition demanding the restricted district be eliminated was presented to city council and sent to Attorney General William Bowser, who asked Tuttle's successor as mayor, Sherwood Herchmer, about local sentiment.

Herchmer was scathing in his response. Admitting he held "decided opinions on this question," he insisted things had been "running along smoothly enough" until the arrival of the mischief-making agitator Dr. Shearer. He insisted the restricted district was "a necessary evil" that could not be done away with, arguing that "the majority of the better element" in Fernie agreed with him.[369] He noted he was unconcerned that the moral reformers had declared this was to be the sole issue in the upcoming annual civic election of 1911. However, the campaign for morality was certainly having an impact. Even the editor of the *Free Press*—who continued to prefer regulation to suppression—conceded it might be time for a change.[370]

But no change occurred. The new mayor and council of 1911 agreed with their predecessors. The census conducted in June of that

A Methodist group on the steps of their church, n.d. Fernie & District Historical Society 6623

year indicates that Pearl Brown had moved on and that two additional brothels were operating either on or adjacent to the approved location on Cokato Road. The fourteen women enumerated in those brothels were comparable to those of a decade earlier. The majority were from the United States, but fewer of them were identified as Black. Others were French, Belgian, Irish and Japanese; just one of Canadian birth is identified. Of the names found in newspapers before 1911 and/or in the census of 1901, only Frankie Smith—the operator of the largest establishment—was still in Fernie.

Local voices calling for an end to tolerance of the brothels persisted and became part of a broad national campaign focusing on alcohol, gambling and prostitution. From modest beginnings in the Presbyterian Church in 1907, the Moral and Social Reform Council of Canada soon included Methodists, Baptists, Congregationalists, the Trades and Labor Congress of Canada, the Church of England and the Salvation Army. The council met annually in Toronto, and its report of 1911 specifically identified Fernie and its brothels as an area of concern:

The cities of Fernie and Cranbrook some time ago drove their respective colonies of social vice outside the city limits, and have since been given the right by the attorney-general of British Columbia to have police jurisdiction over this extra moral colony [of] crime, and are drawing a large revenue in the form of nominal fines from the women concerned.[371]

Pressure from members of the council was persistent. In 1913, following an interview with Fernie's Presbyterian minister, a Toronto newspaper reported that the city needed "cleaning" as it was awash with liquor, gambling and prostitution problems. The fact that teachers' salaries had once been paid largely from fines imposed upon prostitutes was mentioned again. The report raised the ire of the *Free Press*, which commented editorially that Toronto certainly had its share of prostitution and vice and should attend to its own house before calling for a cleansing of Fernie. However, the newspaper did agree that salaries paid by the City of Fernie and any organization receiving a civic grant—from the city band to the Salvation Army— were partially funded by fines levied on prostitutes in police court.[372]

Perhaps as a consequence of the unwelcome publicity, fines nearly doubled for brothel operators in September 1913. In that month, seven such operators—fined $37 each—and their fourteen resident prostitutes—paying fines of $11 each—contributed $413 to city coffers, approximately two-thirds of all fines collected. The answer to Frankie Scouten's question of 1899 about how often she should expect such fines to be levied had long been clear, but this was the first time in nearly a decade that the amount of the monthly fine had been increased. Patrons found visiting "the marts of vice" during the monthly raids also contributed to city coffers, typically paying fines of $6 to $12 for vagrancy or facing a week or two in jail.[373]

The agitation in Fernie for removal of the brothels—like all other concerns—was overwhelmed by matters pertaining to the Great War after August 1914. Ironically, however, it was the war that brought about the success of the moral reform movement in British Columbia. Wrapped in the mantle of patriotism and focusing upon the negative effects of alcohol, the social reformers gathered strength with each passing year, contributing significantly to the success of the prohibition referendum and the election of the province's first Liberal government in late 1916.[374] The new administration announced it would vigorously enforce laws that had been ignored by its predecessors, particularly those laws pertaining to prostitution.

The new policy was soon felt in Fernie, but other communities felt it first. And fundamentally, the change came from without, not from within. Thomas Uphill, mayor since 1915, although a declared Methodist, had little to say on the question, presumably indicating he shared the views of all those who had preceded him in that office. Those views were quickly becoming irrelevant. In February 1917, Chief Constable George Welsby received direct instructions from the superintendent of provincial police in Victoria to improve the moral tone of East Kootenay. Immediately, he ordered the closure of brothels in Michel, Hosmer and Elko, and travelled to Cranbrook to supervise the closing of the restricted district there.[375]

At the *Free Press*, editor John Wallace, who consistently preferred regulation to a policy of repression, commented that the evicted former residents of the restricted district in Cranbrook were "scattered all over the city wherever they could find lodgings and prostitution is known to be more common than ever." The rector of the Church of England in Cranbrook soon urged the "clean-minded public of Fernie" to follow Cranbrook's example. In March, provincial authorities asked police commissioners in Fernie to cooperate, and local ministers of the Presbyterian, Methodist and Anglican churches demanded they do so without delay. The commissioners ordered city police to cooperate with provincial police to accomplish the task, prompting the *Free Press* to note this was "the first time the city has complied with the requests of the leaders of moral reform."[376]

It was, indeed, a watershed moment. Provincial police chief Welsby announced he would allow the brothels one final weekend before closing the restricted district on Monday, March 19. The last raid by city police had occurred at the end of February, with four brothel keepers and eleven prostitutes paying their usual fines on charges of vagrancy. Wallace soon noted that the closure in mid-March brought a result parallel to what had occurred in Cranbrook. He wrote that some of "the inmates left town, some are at hotels, and some have taken rooms around town."[377] During a fractious meeting of city council at the end of the month, the efforts of city police to deal with the new realities were sharply criticized, and a raid on one house re-established in the Annex was discussed. The decision was made to send one prostitute—apparently homeless since the crackdown—to a church-sponsored home in Vancouver, while another, who refused to accept the changed circumstances, was sentenced to six months hard labour by the local police magistrate. [378]

Even months later, anticipating a large attendance at Labour Day events, local ministers of religion urged the police commissioners not to "take off the lid" for the weekend. The commissioners assured them the lid would stay on and announced they had once again permanently closed what was being referred to as "the former red-light district."[379] It was clear that no further revenue from that traditional source on Cokato Road would benefit civic coffers. On the last day of December 1917, the City of Fernie formally relinquished its authority over the Cokato Road location to the provincial police. Chief Welsby went to the restricted district and gave the three prostitutes he found still living there twenty-four hours to leave. In his monthly report for December, he recorded: "Received instructions from Superintendent re taking over old restricted area... Closed it down tight."[380]

Of course, not all the denizens of Cokato Road obediently left Fernie and environs. However, the era of a civically sanctioned red-light district was over. In the local elections of January 1918, supporters of moral and social reform were pleased to see their views represented at last with the election of a sympathetic mayor, of William Dicken as alderman and of police commissioners intent on the strict enforcement of existing laws. And enforce them they did. According to the *Free Press*, when a "bevy of soiled doves" from the United States arrived in Fernie amidst the turmoil surrounding the OBU strike, they were quickly "herded back" across the line by local police.[381] Six months later, George Henderson—founder of the *Free Press* and once the strident critic of the community's tolerance of social vices—became mayor of Fernie. Questions of morality remained, but they were centred upon alcohol and prohibition—not prostitution. Of the "soiled doves" from the still recent past, barely a whisper could be heard.

POSTSCRIPT

History is always replete with ironies. In 1911, miner John Tolley and his family were living in Cokato. According to information gathered by the census taker, they identified then as atheists. By the time the census of 1921 was conducted—four years after the final closing of the restricted district—John and Annie Tolley were declaring themselves Methodist in religion. Presumably needing more space for their growing family, they had moved into the house formerly operated as a brothel by Frankie Smith on Cokato Road. The collection of photographs held at the Fernie Museum includes a poor, ghostly image of that house—an image fittingly appropriate for the chapter of local history that involved Lena Bell, her peers and her critics, a chapter that is now so very difficult to see.

The former brothel on Cokato Road. Fernie & District Historical Society 0173

BIBLIOGRAPHY

NEWSPAPERS

Bellevue Times

Blairmore Enterprise

British Columbia Federationist

Calgary Daily Herald

Coleman Miner

Cranbrook Herald

Creston Review

Daily News Advertiser (Vancouver)

The Despatch (Morrissey)

District Ledger (Fernie)

Fernie Free Press

Frank Paper

Edmonton Bulletin

Edmonton Journal

The Ledge (Fernie)

Lethbridge Daily Herald

Nanaimo Daily News

Nanaimo Free Press

Ottawa Journal

The Financial Post

The Prospector (Fort Steele)

Times-Colonist (Victoria)

Vancouver Province

Vancouver Sun

Vancouver World

Victoria Daily Colonist

Victoria Daily Times

Archival Sources

Royal BC Museum and Archives (RBCMA)

Attorney General, Company Registration Files (1897 series). GR-1438

Attorney General. Correspondence. GR-0429

County Court (Fort Steele) Civil Files. GR 1603

Fort Steele County Court Probate/Estate Files. GR 1619.8

Inspector Provincial Police. GR-97

Provincial Police Force. Clubs Regulations Act. GR-95

Provincial Police Force. GR-0445

Provincial Police Force. Superintendent, Prohibition Files. GR-1425

Provincial Police Force. Superintendent. GR-0057

Sessional Papers. Annual Reports of the Board of Health.

Sessional Papers. Annual Reports of the Liquor Control Board.

Sessional Papers. Annual Reports of the Minister of Mines.

Glenbow Western Research Centre (GWRC)

Crowsnest Resources Limited Fonds.

Crow's Nest Pass Coal Company. M-1561

United Mine Workers of America. District 18 Fonds. M-2239

United Mine Workers of America. District 18 Fonds. M-6000

Library and Archives Canada (LAC)

Census of Canada 1901

Census of Canada 1911

Census of Canada 1921

Department of Justice. RG 13

Immigration Branch. Immigrants from China, 1885–1949. RG 76

Secretary of State. Internment Operations Branch. RG 6

Fernie Museum and Archives (FMA)

City of Fernie Police Book, 1909–1912

City of Fernie Police Record, 1912–1923

Fernie & District Historical Society (FDHS) Photograph Collection

Newspaper Souvenir Publications

Directories

Henderson's British Columbia Gazetteer and Directory 1905

Henderson's British Columbia Gazetteer and Directory 1910, Part One

Jeffries and Co.'s Southeast Kootenay Directory 1914

Wrigley's British Columbia Directory 1918

Wrigley's British Columbia Directory 1920

Wrigley's British Columbia Directory 1921

Books and Articles

Anderson, Frank W. *The Hillcrest Mine Disaster*. Calgary: Frontier Books, 1969.

Buckley, Karen. *Danger, Death and Disaster in the Crowsnest Pass Mines, 1902–1928*. Calgary: University of Calgary Press, 2004.

Campbell, Robert A. *Demon Rum or Easy Money: Government Control of Liquor in British Columbia from Prohibition to Privatization*. Ottawa: Carleton University Press, 1991.

_____ *Sit Down and Drink Your Beer: Regulating Vancouver's Beer Parlours, 1925–1954*. Toronto: University of Toronto Press, 2001.

Cherrington, Ruth. "'We Are Not Drinking Dens!': Working Men's Clubs and the Struggle for Respectability, 1862–1920s." *Brewery History* 153 (2013).

Chow, Lily. *Hard is the Journey: Stories of Chinese Settlement in BC's Kootenays*. Qualicum Beach: Caitlin Press, 2022.

Crowsnest and its People. Coleman, AB: Crowsnest Pass Historical Society, 1979.

Crow's Nest Pass Illustrated. Fernie: Fernie Free Press, 1907.

Fernie, BC: From 1897 to 1903. Fernie: Fernie Free Press, 1902.

Fernie: Souvenir Edition. Fernie: Fernie Free Press, 1901.

Francis, Daniel. *Closing Time: Prohibition, Rum-Runners, and Border Wars*. Madeira Park, BC: Douglas and McIntyre, 2014.

Goutor, David. *Guarding the Gates: The Canadian Labour Movement and Immigration, 1872–1934*. Vancouver: UBC Press, 2008.

Gray, James. *Red Lights on the Prairies*. Saskatoon, SK: Fifth House, 1971.

Hagelund, William A. *House of Suds: A History of Beer Brewing in Western Canada*. Surrey, BC: Hancock House, 2003.

Hamilton, Douglas L. *Sobering Dilemma: A History of Prohibition in British Columbia*. Vancouver: Ronsdale Press, 2004.

Hillcrest Mine Disaster. Coleman, AB: 100th Anniversary Commemoration Committee, 2014.

Johnson, Arthur. *Breaking the Banks*. Toronto: Lester & Orpen Dennys, 1986.

Kordan, Bohdan S. *No Free Man: Canada, the Great War, and the Enemy Alien Experience*. Montreal and Kingston: McGill-Queen's University Press, 2016.

Mayse, Susan. *Ginger: The Life and Death of Albert Goodwin*. Madeira Park, BC: Harbour Publishing, 1990.

McDonald, Robert. "'Simply a Working Man': Tom Uphill of Fernie." In Wayne Norton and Tom Langford, eds. *A World Apart: The Crowsnest Communities of Alberta and British Columbia*. Kamloops, BC: Plateau Press, 2002, pp. 99–112.

McNair, Don. *Vernon Internment Camp, 1914–1920*. Vernon, BC: Vernon Historical Society, 2017.

Nesteroff, Greg. "Boris Karloff in British Columbia." *British Columbia History* 39, no. 1 (2006).

Norris, John. "The Vancouver Island Coal Miners, 1912–1914: A Study of an Organizational Strike." *BC Studies* 45 (1980), pp. 56–72.

Norton, Wayne. "'Fair Manipulators of the Twisted Hickory': Women's Hockey in Fernie, 1919–1926." In Wayne Norton and Naomi Miller, eds. *The Forgotten Side of the Border: British Columbia's Elk Valley and Crowsnest Pass*. Kamloops, BC: Plateau Press, 1998, pp. 206–216.

_____ *Fernie at War: 1914–1919*. Halfmoon Bay, BC: Caitlin Press, 2017.

_____ *Women on Ice: The Early Years of Women's Hockey in Western Canada*. Vancouver: Ronsdale Press, 2009.

Plummer, Kevin. "The Home Bank's House of Cards." *Historicist*, found at https://torontoist.com/2013/08/historicist-the-home-banks-house-of-cards/.

Progressive Fernie. Fernie: District Ledger, 1909.

Roberts, Barbara. *Whence They Came: Deportation from Canada, 1900–1935*. Ottawa: University of Ottawa Press, 1988.

Roy, Patricia E. *A White Man's Province: British Columbia Politicians and Chinese and Japanese Immigrants, 1858–1914*. Vancouver: UBC Press, 1989.

_____ *Boundless Optimism: Richard McBride's British Columbia*. Vancouver: UBC Press, 2012.

Schade, Daniel. "A Militia History of the Occupation of the Vancouver Island Coalfields, August 1913." *BC Studies* 182 (2014), pp. 11–44.

Souvenir Fernie, 1905–06. Fernie: Fernie Free Press, 1905.

Stonebanks, Roger. *Fighting for Dignity: The Ginger Goodwin Story.* St. John's: Canadian Committee on Labour History, 2004.

Yee, Paul. *Saltwater City: An Illustrated History of the Chinese in Vancouver.* Vancouver: Douglas and McIntyre, 1988.

ENDNOTES

HEALTHY, MANLY SPORT

1   *Fernie Free Press*, May 25, 1900, p. 1.

2   *Fernie Free Press*, March 21, 1903, p. 5; April 11, 1903, p. 1.

3   *The Despatch* (Morrissey), May 6, 1904, p. 5.

4   *Fernie Free Press*, May 27, 1904, Supplement, p. 1.

5   *Fernie Free Press*, June 3, 1904, p. 1.

6   *District Ledger*, April 13, 1912, p. 10; April 27, 1903, p. 1.

7   *The Ledge*, July 26, 1905, p. 1.

8   *Crow's Nest Pass Illustrated* (Fernie Free Press, 1907), n.p.

9   *Fernie Free Press*, April 20, 1906, p. 1; *Fernie Ledger*, June 27, 1906, p. 1.

10   *Fernie Free Press*, September 21, 1906, p. 8. With receipts of $83 and admittance typically 25 cents, attendance was well over three hundred.

11   *Frank Paper*, June 25, 1908, p. 4.

12   *District Ledger*, July 25, 1908, p. 2.

13   *District Ledger*, September 25, 1909, p. 1.

14   *District Ledger*, June 25, 1910, p. 5.

15   Roger Stonebanks, *Fighting for Dignity: The Ginger Goodwin Story* (St. John's: Canadian Committee on Labour History, 2004), pp. 25–29; *District Ledger*, October 1, 1910, p. 5. The league medals were placed on display at the Michel branch of the Trites-Wood store in late October. The medals for Goodwin, Arthur Boothman and Tom Carney were likely mailed to them in Cumberland.

16   Only at Coal Creek, where proprieties were often less stringently observed, were women and girls welcomed amongst supporters at games. See, for example, *District Ledger*, June 26, 1909, p. 5.

17   *Fernie Free Press*, November 18, 1910, p. 6; *District Ledger*, November 19, 1910, p. 1; *Cranbrook Herald*, November 17, 1910, p. 8.

18   *Coleman Miner*, November 25, 1910, p. 1.

19   *District Ledger*, April 19, 1913, p. 4.

20   *Crowsnest and Its People* (Coleman, AB: Crowsnest Pass Historical Society, 1979), p. 724.

21   *District Ledger*, September 30, 1911, p. 5; October 14, 1910, pp. 4, 5; October 21, 1910, p. 5.

22   *District Ledger*, March 2, 1912, p. 12.

23   *District Ledger*, March 23, 1912, p. 10; April 6, 1912, p. 1.

24   *District Ledger*, June 8, 1912, p. 5.

25   *Bellevue Times*, February 28, 1913, p. 1.

26   *District Ledger*, April 26, 1913, p. 6.

27 ' *District Ledger*, September 27, 1913, p. 5.

28   *District Ledger*, October 4, 1913, p. 1; October 11, 1913, p. 4.

29   *District Ledger*, October 25, 1913, p. 5. The only note of regret was that long-time Coleman FC secretary Jonathan Graham could not share in the celebration. He died following an operation for appendicitis in August. At his funeral, the cortège—described as the largest ever seen in Coleman—included the entire Coleman Football Club. See *District Ledger*, August 30, 1913, p. 1.

30   *District Ledger*, March 28, 1914, p. 1. Wilson, Gates and Trites were also honorary vice-presidents of Fernie FC in 1914. President of the club was Thomas Biggs, a well-known local socialist and union activist. The game was creating unlikely bedfellows.

31   Like the old ground at Coal Creek, the Corbin football ground possessed a distinct slope. *District Ledger*, August 8, 1914, p. 1.

32   *District Ledger*, April 4, 1914, p. 8.

33   *District Ledger*, May 30, 1914, p. 3. While wonderfully useful, the lists are also incomplete and confusing: incomplete because Bellevue FC is not included; confusing because last-minute additions to several teams are made without identifying the teams at the end of the list of Fernie players.

34   The single exception, Hillcrest FC secretary Joseph Brehler, was German born according to the Canadian census of 1911.

35   *District Ledger*, August 30, 1913, p. 8; May 30, 1914, p. 1; June 6, 1914, pp. 1, 5.

36   *Fernie Free Press*, July 3, 1914, p. 1.

37   Frank W. Anderson, *The Hillcrest Mine Disaster* (Calgary: Frontier Books, 1969), p. 10; *District Ledger*, May 30, 1914, p. 3. *Bellevue Times*, June 26, 1914, p. 4.

38   *District Ledger*, August 1, 1914, p. 1

39   *Blairmore Enterprise*, August 21, 1914, p. 4.

40   *Bellevue Times*, September 4, 1914, p. 8.

41   *The Despatch* (Morrissey), April 15, 1904, p. 5.

From Beirut and Damascus

42 *Fernie Free Press*, October 27, 1905, p. 4.

43 The advertisements appeared in the *Fernie Ledger* from July 25 to September 12, 1906. Michael Boassaly is listed at Fernie for the first time in *Henderson's British Columbia Gazetteer and Directory 1905*.

44 *District Ledger*, October 17, 1908, p. 1.

45 Jeffries and Co.'s *Southeast Kootenay Directory 1914*, p. 76: *Fernie Free Press*, July 30, 1909, p. 1.

46 Although born in Damascus, Frank Kefoury is identified as Greek rather than Syrian in the 1911 census. After 1911, references to this family consistently use the spelling Kafoury.

47 Hosmer also attracted several Syrian merchants. Michael Boassaly had moved from Fernie to Hosmer by 1911. The 1911 census for Hosmer is very difficult to read. Two small families identified as Syrian have surnames that are illegible. The more legible surnames, in addition to Rahal and Boassaly, seem to be Ghiz and Ezzy.

48 *Fernie Free Press*, March 19, 1909, p. 5. William is recorded as a local farmer in the 1911 census. Curiously, the 1911 census identifies the religion of the Haddad family in Fernie as Presbyterian!

49 *Henderson's British Columbia Gazetteer and Directory 1910, Part 1*, p. 766; *District Ledger*, April 30, 1910, p. 3. Merchants with the surname Haddad are also at this time found in Lethbridge and Spokane. In Cranbrook, Solomon Koury and family followed the same path as the Kfoury family, immigrating to Quebec around the turn of the century and moving west some years later.

50 *Vancouver Sun*, October 12, 1924; reprinted in *Fernie Free Press*, October 17, 1924, p. 2.

51 Both Joseph and Khalil Saad were married in Fernie during the first few months of the Great War. Khalil's bride was Nezera Joseph, daughter of his Syrian neighbours Albert and Lena Joseph. According to census data, Khalil first arrived in Canada in 1900 and Nezera in 1914.

52 *District Ledger*, July 11, 1914, p. 7.

53 *District Ledger*, September 13, 1913, p. 1; *Vancouver Province*, October 1, 1913, p. 4; *Vancouver Daily World*, October 2, p. 9; *Fernie Free Press*, October 31, 1913, p. 4.

54 *Semi-Weekly Spokesman-Review* (Spokane), October 29, 1914, p. 7; *Blairmore Enterprise*, November 6, 1914, p. 8.

55 *District Ledger*, January 2, 1915, p. 1; March 5, 1915, p. 1.

56 For 1918, for example, see *Fernie Free Press*, April 26, pp. 1, 2; November 15, p. 1; and November 22, pp. 1, 2.

57 *Lethbridge Herald*, September 24, 1919, p. 1; *Fernie Free Press*, September 26, 1919, p. 1; *Vancouver Sun*, October 6, 1919, p. 3.

58   *Calgary Herald*, May 20, 1919, p. 3; *District Ledger*, August 1, 1919, p. 4.

59   *Blairmore Enterprise*, June 10, 1920, p. 8; October 7, 1920, p. 8. James Haddad left Bellevue to become a boot and shoe salesman in Vancouver; his brother Edward moved to Winnipeg.

60   *Fernie Free Press*, September 30, 1921, p. 5. The census of 1921 indicates that another Syrian salesman, Anthony Abide, was boarding with the Yohnis family. Abide was likely a local resident much earlier, having been a witness to the Saad-Joseph marriage in Fernie in 1915.

61   When Arnfly Kefoury died in Vancouver in 1930 at the age of 116—having outlived her son Nassif by five years—she was thought to have been the oldest person in Canada. See *Vancouver Sun*, March 13, 1930, p. 20. Reports of her death appeared in newspapers across the continent.

On Stage Tonight

62   Greg Nesteroff, "Boris Karloff in British Columbia," *British Columbia History* 39, no. 1 (2006), p. 19. In published lists of cash donations to the Fernie District Fire Relief Fund, the $700 raised by the Russell troupe's benefit performance is included in the total of $799 received from Edmonton. See, for example, the list of donations in the *District Ledger*, January 30, 1909, p. 5.

63   *District Ledger*, November 20, 1909, pp. 4, 8; *Fernie Free Press*, November 26, 1909, p. 8.

64   *District Ledger*, December 4, 1909, pp. 4, 6, 8; *Fernie Free Press*, December 4, 1909, p. 8.

65   The new name resolved the confusion around identifying the new theatre as the Fernie Opera House (a name used for years and still claimed by the long-established Fernie opera house), the Miners' Opera House and the Grand Opera House, but it may have been adopted simply to avoid the possessive case. Since its opening in October 1909, the venue had advertised itself (and had been referred to in newspaper comment) as the Miner Theatre, the Miner's Theatre, the Miner's Union Theatre, the Miners' Union Theatre, the Miner's Opera House and the Miners Opera House. The Grand must have seemed so much simpler.

66   *District Ledger*, January 29, 1910, pp. 1, 5; February 5, 1910, p. 5.

67   *District Ledger*, February 17, 1912, p. 8.

68   *Fernie Free Press*, February 16, 1912, pp. 1, 3, 5; *District Ledger*, February 17, 1912, p. 8. The performance of *Emanuella* at the Blairmore Opera House on February 28 generated a similar appraisal. See *Blairmore Enterprise*, February 29, 1912, p. 4.

69   Greg Nesteroff, "Boris Karloff in British Columbia," *British Columbia History* 39, no. 1 (2006), p. 20; Stephen Jacobs, "Boris Karloff in Alberta," *Alberta History* 55, no. 22 (2007), found at http://www.morethanamonster.com/downloads/Boris-Karloff-in-Alberta.pdf.

SEDITION AT MICHEL

70 Glenbow Western Research Centre, Crow's Nest Pass Coal Company Employee Records Series 9, M-1561-425 (Michel Colliery "E" 1911–1916); *District Ledger*, January 20, 1912, p. 5.

71 *District Ledger*, February 24, 1912, pp. 1, 6; March 2, 1912, p. 6; April 4, 1912, p. 5; September 28, 1912, p. 3.

72 *District Ledger*, December 30, 1912, p. 1.

73 Annual Report of the Minister of Mines for the Year Ending 31st December 1912, RBCMA, British Columbia, Sessional Papers 1913, K 316.

74 *District Ledger*, December 28, 1912, p. 1; July 12, 1913, p. 5; August 9, 1913, pp. 1, 5.

75 John Norris, "The Vancouver Island Coal Miners, 1912–1914: A Study of an Organizational Strike," *BC Studies* 45 (1980), pp. 56–72; Daniel Schade, "A Militia History of the Occupation of the Vancouver Island Coalfields, August 1913," *BC Studies* 182 (2014), pp. 11–44.

76 *District Ledger*, September 20, 1913, p. 4.

77 *British Columbia Federationist*, February 20, 1914, p. 1.

78 *District Ledger*, March 7, 1914, p. 5.

79 *District Ledger*, March 14, 1914, p. 1.

80 *District Ledger*, April 4, 1914, p. 4; April 11, 1914, p. 8.

81 *District Ledger*, April 4, 1914, p. 1.

82 *District Ledger*, April 25, 1914, p. 5.

83 Elmer and the other delegate, David Rees, wrote a joint report to that effect on their return from the Rocky Mountain Convention; the report was submitted by Rees to the District 18 annual meeting several months later. See *District Ledger*, February 20, 1915, p. 7. For delegate appointments, see *District Ledger*, May 30, 1914, p. 4.

84 For the strike in Colorado and the involvement of the militia, see the *District Ledger* throughout 1914, https://www.britannica.com/event/Ludlow-Massacre, and Elliot Gorn, *Mother Jones: The Most Dangerous Woman in America* (New York: Hill and Wang, 2001).

85 *Hillcrest Mine Disaster* (Coleman, AB: 100th Anniversary Commemoration Committee, 2014). For contemporary reports, see the weekly issues of the *District Ledger* and the *Fernie Free Press* for the end of June and throughout July 1914. See also Karen Buckley, *Danger, Death and Disaster in the Crowsnest Pass Mines, 1902–1928* (Calgary: University of Calgary Press, 2004).

86 *District Ledger*, August 1, 1914, pp. 1, 4.

87 *District Ledger*, August 8, 1914, p. 4.

88   *District Ledger,* August 15, 1914, p. 4.

89   *District Ledger,* August 29, 1914, p. 4.

90   Bohdan S. Kordan, *No Free Man: Canada, the Great War, and the Enemy Alien Experience* (Montreal and Kingston: McGill-Queen's University Press, 2016), pp. 44–55 and 268–274.

91   *District Ledger,* September 26, 1914, p. 5.

92   *Fernie Free Press,* September 18, 1914, p. 5; *District Ledger,* September 26, 1914, p. 8, and October 3, 1914, p. 5.

93   *British Columbia Federationist,* October 16, 1914, p. 3.

94   William Ridgway Wilson to A.P. Sherwood, Chief Commissioner of Police, December 10, 1914, LAC, Department of Justice, RG 13-A-2, vol. 190, file 1915-33. For his attitude to Canadians with names of German origin, see William Ridgway Wilson to Major General Otter, July 2, 1918, LAC, RG 6, Internment Operations, vol. 764, file 5044 (part II), Personnel, Officers in Camps of B.C. (1916–1918), and Wayne Norton with Ella Verkerk, "Communities Divided: The Internment Camps of World War One," in *The Forgotten Side of the Border,* eds. Wayne Norton and Naomi Miller (Kamloops, BC: Plateau Press, 1998), p. 88.

95   *British Columbia Federationist,* October 16, 1914, p. 3; David Rees to Deputy Minister of Justice, December 2, 1918, LAC, Department of Justice, RG 13-A-2, vol. 229, file 1918-2566. Interestingly, Welsby made no reference to a military order to arrest Elmer in his official report, preferring to take credit for independent action. Welsby to Colin Campbell, October 6, 1914, RBCMA, Provincial Police Force, Superintendent, 1912–1922, GR-0057, box 21, file 13.

96   *Fernie Free Press,* October 2, 1914, p. 1.

97   *District Ledger,* October 10, 1914, p. 5.

98   *District Ledger,* October 10, 1914, pp. 1, 4.

99   For the history of the camp at Vernon, see Don McNair, *Vernon Internment Camp 1914–1920* (Vernon, BC: Vernon Historical Society, 2017).

100   David Rees to Deputy Minister of Justice, December 2, 1918, LAC, Department of Justice, RG 13-A-2, vol. 229, file 1918-2566.

101   *British Columbia Federationist,* February 5, 1915, p. 2; *Lethbridge Herald,* February 6, 1915, p. 1.

102   *District Ledger,* February 27, 1915, p. 1. Rees at this time believed only one man had complained to Major Wilson, but subsequently noted that two had done so.

103   Lt.-Col. MacPherson to Deputy Minister of Justice, March 9, 1915, LAC, Department of Justice, RG 13-A-2, vol. 192, file 1915-419.

104   Bohdan S. Kordan, *No Free Man: Canada, the Great War, and the Enemy Alien Experience* (Montreal and Kingston: McGill-Queen's University Press, 2016), p. 236.

105   David Rees to Deputy Minister of Justice, December 2, 1918; Major General Otter to Deputy Minister of Justice, December 10, 1918, LAC, Department of Justice, RG 13-A-2, vol. 229, file 1918-2566.

106   Barbara Roberts, *Whence They Came: Deportation from Canada, 1900–1935* (Ottawa: University of Ottawa Press, 1988), pp. 73–83.

107   Sir William Otter, *Report on Internment Operations, 1914–1919* (Ottawa, 1921), p. 14; file "Deported Enemy Nationals," p. 9, LAC, Department of the Secretary of State, RG 6, vol. 771.

Doris and Dahlia

108   Wayne Norton, *Fernie at War: 1914–1919* (Halfmoon Bay, BC: Caitlin Press, 2017), pp. 160–162.

109   "'Fair Manipulators of the Twisted Hickory': Women's Hockey in Fernie, 1919–1926," in *The Forgotten Side of the Border*, eds. Wayne Norton and Naomi Miller (Plateau Press: Kamloops, 1998), pp. 206–216, and Wayne Norton, *Women on Ice: The Early Years of Women's Hockey in Western Canada* (Ronsdale Press: Vancouver, 2009).

110   Wayne Norton, *Fernie at War: 1914–1919* (Halfmoon Bay, BC: Caitlin Press, 2017), p. 136.

111   Although no games were subsequently reported, the Fernie Ladies Hockey Team in 1909 challenged their counterparts in Cranbrook. See *Fernie Free Press*, February 5, 1909, p. 1.

112   That roster included nearly all the names that would form the basis of local women's hockey for years to come: Bertha Whalley, Doris Henderson, Dahlia Schagel, Edith Biggs, Mary Dragon and Dorothy Hamill. Nancy Wood and Mrs. Evelyn Donaldson were also included in this initial roster. See *District Ledger*, February 6, 1919, p. 1.

113   *District Ledger*, March 7, 1919, p. 1. The sports editor at the *District Ledger* provided detailed, page-one coverage of local women's hockey in 1919.

114   It is worth noting that another innovation occurred at Fernie in 1921 when the Bank of Commerce team—formed to meet a challenge from the combined Home and Imperial banks—included three women (Nancy Wood, Mary Dragon and Ella Fenwick), all members of the emerging women's team. *Fernie Free Press*, February 18, 1921, p. 1.

115   *Fernie Free Press*, November 11, 1921, p. 4; November 18, 1921, p. 5.

116   *Fernie Free Press*, May 5, 1922, p. 2.

117   *Calgary Herald*, January 23, 1922, p. 16.

118   *Calgary Herald*, January 23, 1922, p. 16; *District Ledger*, February 6, 1919, p. 1.

119   The team roster at Banff consisted of Jessie Richardson, Dahlia Schagel, Doris Henderson, Elaine Ross, Edith Biggs, Florence Hamill, Mrs. Bishop Wilson (née Ella Fenwick), Mary Dragon and Belva Graves.

120   Such a mascot would have raised few eyebrows in 1923. In April, a play writ-ten by the public school principal played to a packed house at the Grand Theatre. It included six students performing roles in blackface. See *Lethbridge Herald*, April 7, 1923, p. 7.

121   *Fernie Free Press*, March 9, 1923, p. 1; *Calgary Herald*, March 12, 1923, p. 5.

122   With the exception of Elaine Ross, the team of 1924 was the same as that of 1923. A player identified only as Miss Muir replaced Elaine Ross.

123   *Fernie Free Press*, May 30, 1924, pp. 1, 5.

124   The team did find a new local opponent in the Cranbrook Canucks; one of the new players for the Swastikas was Dahlia's younger sister, Althea Schagel. See *Cranbrook Herald*, February 26, 1925, p. 7; *Fernie Free Press*, February 27, 1925, p. 8.

125   *Fernie Free Press*, January 6, 1958, p. 4; January 30, 1958, p. 2.

Tattered Dreams

126   The club, its members and newspaper reporters often referred to the "Work-ingman's Club." Most frequently, it was identified as the "Workingmen's Club" and that usage has been followed here.

127   Ruth Cherrington, "'We Are Not Drinking Dens!': Working Men's Clubs and the Struggle for Respectability, 1862–1920s," *Brewery History* 153 (2013), pp. 11–20.

128   *District Ledger*, January 30, 1909, p. 4.

129   Wayne Norton and William Milburn, "The Coal Creek Literary and Athletic Association Clubhouse," in *The Forgotten Side of the Border*, eds. Wayne Norton and Naomi Miller (Kamloops, BC: Plateau Press, 1998), pp. 185–188.

130   *Fernie Free Press*, May 20, 1904, p. 1.

131   *District Ledger*, January 25, 1908, p. 4; February 15, 1908, p. 8.

132   *District Ledger*, May 9, 1908, p. 6.

133   *District Ledger*, August 8, 1908, p. 1: *Cranbrook Herald*, August 13, 1908, p. 1.

134   RBCMA, Attorney General Registrar General, Society Series, GR 1438, file 221. Incorporating under the name "Gladstone Local Union No. 2314, UMWA," the society stated its purpose was to provide benefits for survivors of men killed in mining accidents. There is no mention in the incorporation docu-ments of the Miners' Union Building. See also *District Ledger*, February 13, 1909, p. 5; March 12, 1910, p. 7.

135   *District Ledger*, August 21, 1909, p. 1

136   McMullin to Hussey, May 21, 1909, RBCMA, GR-95, file 2, BC Provincial Po-lice, Clubs Regulations Act, vol. 1, Correspondence 1909–1910.

137   Eckstein to Superintendent Hussey, June 4, 1909, Provincial Police, Clubs

Regulations Act, vol. 1, Correspondence 1909–1910, GR-95, file 2, RBCMA, British Columbia, Registrar General, Society Series, GR-1438, file 227.

138 *District Ledger*, November 6, 1909, p. 6; Gladstone Local Union Minutes, p. 219, GWRC, UMWA Fonds, M6000, B65, F851. Although located just across the street, the *Free Press* provided no coverage of the Miners' Union Building opening.

139 *Michel Reporter*, December 25, 1909, p. 8.

140 Eckstein to Superintendent Provincial Police, January 1, 1910, GR-95, file 2, RBCMA, BC Provincial Police, Clubs Regulations Act, vol. 1, Correspondence 1909–1910; *District Ledger*, January 8, 1910, pp. 1, 4.

141 *Fernie Free Press*, February 2, 1906, p. 5; June 15, 1906, p. 1.

142 *District Ledger*, February 26, 1910, p. 1; March 12, 1910, p. 7.

143 J.H. McMullin to F.S. Hussey, Inspector Provincial Police, December 22, 1909, RBCMA, GR-97, vol. 1, J.H. McMullin Inspections, January 1909–December 1909.

144 *Fernie Free Press*, January 7, 1910, p. 1; *District Ledger*, February 26, 1910, p. 1.

145 *District Ledger*, August 13, 1910, p. 8.

146 Colin Campbell to F.S. Hussey, November 15, 1910, GR-97, vol. 2, RBCMA, BC Police, Inspector Colin Campbell, Correspondence Inward and Reports; *District Ledger*, January 21, 1911, p. 4.

147 Gladstone Local Union Minutes, p. 95, GWRC, UMWA Fonds, M6000, B65, F851.

148 Gladstone Local Union Minutes, p. 120, GWRC, UMWA Fonds, M6000, B65, F851; "Report of District President," *District Ledger*, February 21, 1914, p. 4.

149 Gladstone Local Union Minutes, p. 219, GWRC, UMWA Fonds, M6000, B65, F851; *District Ledger*, October 12, 1912, p. 8.

150 *District Ledger*, February 21, 1914, p. 4.

151 *District Ledger*, October 11, 1913, p. 1. The advertisements appeared weekly throughout November and December.

152 *Fernie Free Press*, August 1, 1913, p. 5; Gladstone Local Union Minutes, pp. 276, 285, GWRC, UMWA Fonds, M6000, B65, F851.

153 *District Ledger*, February 27, 1915, p. 1.

154 *Fernie Free Press*, February 27, 1914, p. 1.

155 *District Ledger*, May 8, 1915, p. 1; *Fernie Free Press*, May 14, 1915, p. 1.

156 *Fernie Free Press*, April 27, 1917, p. 5; July 27, 1917, p. 5; August 2, 1918, p. 5.

157 *Wrigley's British Columbia Directory, 1918*; *Fernie Free Press*, July 20, 1917, p. 2.

158 *Fernie Free Press*, October 19, 1917, p. 1.

159   *Fernie Free Press*, January 17, 1919, p. 5.

160   *District Ledger*, April 18, 1919, p. 8.

161   *Cranbrook Herald*, August 28, 1919, p. 1. For an analysis of the OBU strike, see Wayne Norton, *Fernie at War: 1914–1919*, pp. 168–180.

162   Statement of Accounts Payable re Miners' Hall, Fernie, BC, GWRC, UMWA Fonds, Series 29, M2239, B15, F140.

163   *Fernie Free Press*, May 7, 1920, p. 1.

164   Statement of Accounts Payable re Miners' Hall, Fernie, BC, GWRC, UMWA Fonds, Series 29, M2239, B15, F140.

165   Financial Statement (1922) and Auditor's Report and Statement (1924), GWRC, UMWA Fonds, Series 29, M6000, B30, F432 and F434.

166   For the same offence, hotels in Fernie and elsewhere were typically fined $300. See Ronald Greene, "The Early Tokens of Fernie, B.C.," in *Numismatica Canada* (Canadian Numismatic Research Society, 2012), p. 95.

167   *Fernie Free Press*, October 3, 1930, p. 1; December 13, 1931, p. 1.

168   *Fernie Free Press*, February 21, 1946, p. 1; May 22, 1947, p. 1.

169   *Cranbrook Herald*, August 28, 1919, p. 1.

EMPIRE OF SUDS

170   Albert Mutz is clearly identifiable in the photograph of Puget Sound Brewery workers and draymen found in Gary Flynn's "History of the Pacific Brewing & Malting Co. of Tacoma." See www.brewerygems.com/pacific.htm.

171   The first reference to Mutz locally is found in *The Prospector* (Fort Steele), February 6, 1896, p. 5.

172   William A. Hagelund, *House of Suds: A History of Beer Brewing in Western Canada* (Surrey, BC: Hancock House, 2003), p. 58.

173   *Fernie Free Press Souvenir Edition*, 1905–1906.

174   *Fernie Free Press*, August 23, 1902, p. 5; *Fernie Free Press Souvenir Edition, 1902*. There is no local historical record of a "branch brewery" having operated at Frank, and no mention of it in company advertising after 1902. Curiously, one newspaper reported it to be in operation in 1905. See *Fernie Free Press*, April 21, 1905, p. 1.

175   *Calgary Herald*, August 23, 1902, p. 7; February 11, 1903, p. 3; *Edmonton Bulletin*, December 12, 1902, p. 5; *The Prospector* (Fort Steele), December 12, 1903, p. 1.

176   RBCMA, Attorney General, Company Registration Files (1897 series), GR-1438, file 1070. The company incorporated with 750 shares valued at $200 each. Mutz and Scott maintained control by holding and equally dividing 405 shares. See also *Fernie Free Press*, January 16, 1904, p. 5.

177   *Cranbrook Herald*, July 9, 1903, p. 2.

178   *Morrissey Despatch*, Friday, May 13, 1904, p. 5; *The Prospector* (Fort Steele), July 30, 1904, p. 1.

179   *The Ledge*, April 26, 1905, p. 1; May 10, 1905, pp. 1, 4; RBCMA, Attorney General, Company Registration Files (1897 series), GR-1438, file 1070. Combining figures from these sources, it seems Eschwig and Jennings each received $3,500 for their quarter-shares of the business, while Klausman received $4,000 for his half-share.

180   *The Ledge*, May 3, 1905, p. 1; *Fernie Free Press*, May 5, 1905, p. 4.

181   *Fernie Free Press*, April 21, 1905, p. 1; May 5, 1905, p. 4; May 26, 1905, p. 4.

182   *The Ledge*, February 22, 1905, p. 1.

183   Scott is not listed by *Henderson's Gazetteer and Directory* as a resident of Fernie after 1904. He is last mentioned in company records in 1906 and is identified then as a rancher at Gateway.

184   *Cranbrook Herald*, February 15, 1906, p. 5. According to the newspaper report, he initially stated he would "operate the plant to its full capacity."

185   For Fritz Sick's full career, see William A. Hagelund, *House of Suds: A History of Beer Brewing in Western Canada*, pp. 51–86. Sick's business empire would eventually include breweries and hotels in Saskatchewan, Alberta, British Columbia and Washington State. See also see *Lethbridge Herald*, July 17, 1908, p. 3.

186   *Fernie Ledger*, July 4, 1906, pp. 3, 4.

187   *Fernie Ledger*, October 31, 1906, p. 4; *Calgary Herald*, November 2, 1906, p. 11.

188   The Fernie-Fort Steele Brewing Company was registered in May 1907, with 4,000 shares valued at $100 each. Mutz was the largest shareholder with 719 shares. RBCMA, Attorney General, Company Registration Files (1897 series), GR-1438, file 1765.

189   *Frank Paper*, August 8, 1907, p. 1.

190   *Fernie Free Press*, December 6, 1907, p. 8; *District Ledger*, June 13, 1908, p. 1. Years later, when Meier was visiting from Butte, Montana, it was reported he had invented a patent bung for beer kegs that made him "a nice bunch of money" while he was employed at the brewery in Fernie. See *Fernie Free Press*, December 9, 1927, p. 5.

191   *District Ledger*, May 9, 1908, p. 1; May 21, 1908, p. 4; *Frank Paper*, July 9, 1908, p. 4.

192   *Coleman Miner*, August 7, 1908, p. 1; *District Ledger*, August 8, 1908, p. 1; *Fernie Free Press*, August 14, 1908, p. 1.

193   *District Ledger*, August 15, 1908, p. 2.

194   *Fernie Free Press*, April 23, 1909, p. 1.

195   *Fernie Free Press*, July 30, 1909, p. 1.

196   *Cranbrook Herald,* August 5, 1909, p. 1; *District Ledger,* August 7, 1909, p. 1.

197   *Fernie Free Press,* August 6, 1909, p. 5; *District Ledger,* August 14, 1909, pp. 1, 2; August 21, 1909, p. 1.

198   *Frank Paper,* September 2, 1909, p. 4.

199   *Coleman Miner,* May 26, 1911, p. 5; *Bellevue Times,* March 19, 1915, p. 8; May 14, 1915, p. 1.

200   Shares were registered in the name of his wife, Alice Mutz. RBCMA, Attorney General, Company Registration Files (1897 series), GR-1438, file 2185; *District Ledger,* August 19, 1911, p. 8.

201   The Vulcan and District Historical Society notes Mutz called the hotel at Vulcan the Imperial because that name was on the chinaware transported from his Imperial Hotel at Frank.

202   *Fernie Free Press,* November 14, 1913, p. 5.

203   *Fernie Free Press,* August 21 to September 18, 1914.

204   The advertisements appear weekly in the *District Ledger* from May to July 1915 and in the *Fernie Free Press* from August to December 1915.

205   RBCMA, Attorney General, Company Registration Files (1897 series), GR-1438, file 1765. On behalf of shareholders, Thomas Crahan sued director Roland Wood for fraud. See *Vancouver Daily World,* December 22, 1915, p. 8.

206   For the tumultuous history of the Elk Valley/Crowsnest region during the prohibition years, see Daniel Francis, *Closing Time: Prohibition, Rum-Runners and Border Wars* (Madeira Park, BC: Douglas and McIntyre, 2014), pp. 87–91, and Wayne Norton, *Fernie at War: 1914–1919* (Halfmoon Bay, BC: Caitlin Press, 2017).

207   Report of Inspector Owen, June 1919, RBCMA, British Columbia, Provincial Police Force, GR-0445, box 51, file 17.

208   *Fernie Free Press,* September and October 1921.

209   RBCMA, Attorney General, Company Registration Files (1897 series), GR-1438, file 2185.

210   *Fernie Free Press,* September 16, 1921, p. 5; *Creston Review,* September 23, 1921, p. 5.

211   *The Financial Post,* June 17, 1950, p. 5.

Solidand Managed with Rigid Conservatism

212   *Fernie Free Press,* May 11, 1906, p. 1; July 6, 1906, p. 3.

213   *Fernie Ledger,* August 1, 1906, p. 1.

214   *Fernie Free Press,* May 13, 1910, p. 1; *District Ledger,* October 1, 1910, p. 1; October 8, 1910, p. 1.

215   The *Fernie Free Press* in those days always printed annual reports from banks with branches in Fernie. This one appeared in the issue of July 6, p. 3.

216   *Fernie Free Press*, August 24, 1923, p. 1.   ·

217   *Fernie Free Press*, August 31, 1923, p. 1; *Vancouver Sun*, September 1, 1923, p. 2.

218   *Nanaimo Daily News*, August 18, 1923, p. 1; *Fernie Free Press*, October 26, 1923, p. 1.

219   *Calgary Herald*, September 1, 1923, p. 15; *Blairmore Enterprise*, September 6, 1923, p. 10. The statistics were provided to Alberta premier Herbert Greenfield at the end of November. It was reported earlier that famed bootlegger Emilio Picariello left small accounts at both the Blairmore and Fernie branches of the Home Bank. See *Calgary Herald*, October 23, 1923, p. 1; November 27, 1923, p. 7.

220   *Fernie Free Press*, October 5, 1923, p. 1; November 9, 1923, p. 5.

221   *Blairmore Enterprise,* October 4, 1923, p. 1. The full list of deposits in western Canadian branches is found here.

222   *Saturday Night* article, reprinted in *Fernie Free Press*, October 19, 1923, p. 2

224   *Fernie Free Press*, October 19, 1923, pp. 4, 8; *Blairmore Enterprise*, November 1, 1923, p. 9. Ironically, as secretary of the Blairmore Hockey Club, bank manager William Bird had to deliver that news at a team meeting.

224   *Calgary Herald*, October 20, 1923, p. 18; *Fernie Free Press*, October 19, 1923, pp. 1, 2.

225   *The Province* (Vancouver), October 25, 1923, p. 2; *Fernie Free Press*, October 26, 1923, p. 1. There were probably only three men in Fernie in 1923 who could afford to foot the bill for the Coal Creek representative. One of them, CNPCC president William Wilson, was known for such acts of generosity.

226   *Fernie Free Press*, October 26, 1923, p. 8; *Edmonton Journal*, October 27, 1923, p. 1. Smith was president of District 18 from June 1913 until June 1914.

227   *Calgary Herald*, November 2, 1923, p. 17. Their counterparts in Calgary rejected motions calling for withdrawals from all chartered banks and for the creation of banks operated by government. See *Calgary Herald*, November 24, 1923, p. 16.

228   *Victoria Daily Times*, October 29, p. 7; November 6, 1923, p. 11; *The Province* (Vancouver), November 6, 1923, p. 2.

229   *Victoria Daily Times*, October 23, 1923, p. 1; *Fernie Free Press*, November 9, 1923, p. 5.

230   *Fernie Free Press*, November 30, 1923, p. 1; December 7, 1923, p. 1.

231   *Fernie Free Press*, December 14, 1923, p. 1

232   *Calgary Herald*, December 15, 1923, p. 16; *Fernie Free Press*, December 14, 1923, pp. 1, 2.

233 *Blairmore Enterprise*, December 20, 1923, p. 20; *The Province* (Vancouver), December 22, 1923, p. 7.

234 *Calgary Herald,* April 27, 1925, p. 1. Arthur Johnson, *Breaking the Banks* (Toronto: Lester & Orpen Dennys, 1986), p. 3; Kevin Plummer, "The Home Bank's House of Cards," in *Historicist,* found at https://torontoist.com/2013/08/historicist-the-home-banks-house-of-cards/.

235 *Fernie Free Press*, January 4, 1924, p. 1.

236 *Fernie Free Press*, January 25, 1924, p. 1.

237 *The Gazette* (Montreal), April 21, 1924, p. 8.

238 *Fernie Free Press*, May 30, 1924, p. 5.

239 *Blairmore Enterprise*, January 17, 1924, p. 1. The form depositors were asked to submit to the liquidators authorizing the payment appeared in the *Calgary Herald*, December 21, 1923, p. 13.

240 Arthur Johnson, *Breaking the Banks* (Toronto: Lester & Orpen Dennys, 1986), p. 12.

241 *Fernie Free Press*, August 1, 1924, pp. 1, 2.

242 *Ottawa Journal*, March 28, 1924, p. 7.

243 *Fernie Free Press*, October 31, 1924, pp. 1, 2; *Calgary Herald*, October 30, 1924, p. 9.

244 *Calgary Herald*, February 16, 1925, p. 5.

246 *The Province* (Vancouver), January 7, 1925, p. 25.

246 W.T.J. Lee and I.E. Weldon, National Executive Committee to Depositor, March 1925. Ronald Greene Collection.

247 *Fernie Free Press*, July 3, 1925, p. 6; *Blairmore Enterprise*, November 25, 1926, p. 5.

248 *Fernie Free Press*, September 4, 1925, p. 4.

249 *Fernie Free Press*, August 28, 1925, p. 4; *Times-Colonist* (Victoria), October 2, 1925, p. 3.

250 *Fernie Free Press*, September 25, 1925, p. 5; November 6, 1925, p. 4; December 4, 1925, p. 5; *Blairmore Enterprise*, October 22, 1925, p. 1; November 5, 1925, p. 1; December 21, 1925, p. 9.

251 *Fernie Free Press*, December 11, 1925, p. 1. John "Jack" Henderson fell to his death attempting to escape from the Hollywood Sanitarium in New Westminster. See *Vancouver Sun*, December 8, 1925, p. 18.

252 *Calgary Herald*, December 5, 1927, p. 13.

253 *Fernie Free Press*, March 4, 1927, p. 4.

254 *Fernie Free Press*, December 9, 1927, p. 5; December 23, 1927, pp. 4, 8.

255 *Fernie Free Press*, December 30, 1927, pp. 1, 4; January 13, 1928, p. 4; January 20, 1928, p. 4.

256 *Fernie Free Press*, December 30, 1927, pp. 1, 4. The seven unpaid depositors who did not sign the letter of support from Caulfield et al. preferred perhaps not to make their names public or may have disagreed with the letter's contents.

257 *Fernie Free Press*, May 25, 1928, p. 1. It is unlikely Dr. King would have been concerned with figures for Blairmore depositors, so it can be assumed this amount was indeed intended for Fernie branch depositors.

258 *Fernie Free Press*, September 14, 1928, p. 1; *Calgary Herald*, October 2, 1928, p. 13. If the number of claims mentioned by Higginbotham is accepted, Henderson's work was not confined exclusively to Fernie and Blairmore.

259 *Fernie Free Press*, January 25, 1929, p. 1. If the surnames published are representative, the Home Bank branch at Fernie evidently attracted depositors from the British, Italian and Eastern European communities.

260 *Fernie Free Press*, January 11, 1929, p. 4; *Blairmore Enterprise*, May 9, 1929, p. 10.

Lee Something or Other...

261 Paul Yee, *Saltwater City: An Illustrated History of the Chinese in Vancouver* (Vancouver: Douglas and McIntyre, 1988); Patricia E. Roy, *A White Man's Province: British Columbia Politicians and Chinese and Japanese Immigrants, 1858–1914* (Vancouver: UBC Press, 1989). Smaller communities have also received attention. See, for example, Liping Wong Yip, *From Wah Lee to Chew Keen: The Story of a Pioneer Chinese Family in North Cariboo* (Altona, MB: Friesen Press, 2017) and, especially, books by Lily Chow: *Sojourners in the North, Blossoms in Gold Mountains: Chinese Settlements in the Fraser Canyon and the Okanagan, Chasing Their Dreams* and *Hard is the Journey: Stories of Chinese Settlement in BC's Kootenays*, all published by Caitlin Press.

262 *Fernie Free Press*, September 29, 1899, p. 5.

263 *Fernie Free Press*, May 11, 1900, p. 8; June 22, 1900, p. 1.

264 *Fernie Free Press*, September 21, 1900, p. 5.

265 *Fernie Free Press*, July 13, 1900, p. 4; September 28, 1900, p. 4.

266 *Fernie Free Press*, March 1, 1901, p. 4.

267 *Cranbrook Herald*, July 12, 1900, p. 4; *Fernie Free Press*, March 1, 1901, p. 4; June 21, 1901, p. 4.

268 *Fernie Free Press*, July 26, 1901, pp. 1, 4.

269 *Fernie Free Press*, June 21, 1902, p. 1; April 25, 1903, p. 1; August 15, 1903, p. 4; *The Ledge*, December 21, 1904, p. 1.

270 *Fernie Free Press*, April 29, 1904, p. 1; May 6, 1904, p. 1.

271 *Fernie Free Press*, August 6, 1909, p. 5.

272 *The Ledge*, March 29, 1905, p. 1; *Fernie Free Press*, August 18, 1905, p. 5; April 23,

1909, p. 5.

273 *Fernie Free Press*, June 16, 1905, p. 1; FMA, City of Fernie Police Book, 1909–1912.

274 Patricia E. Roy, *A White Man's Province: British Columbia Politicians and Chinese and Japanese Immigrants, 1858–1914* (Vancouver: UBC Press, 1989), p. 253.

275 *Fernie Free Press*, April 18, 1903, p. 5; June 6, 1903, p. 5; June 27, 1905, p. 5; *Nelson Daily News*, June 23, 1903, p. 1.

276 *District Ledger*, February 13, 1909, p. 6; February 15, 1909, p. 1.

277 *District Ledger*, February 13, 1909, pp. 4, 6. For the resistance to the employment of Asian labour, see David Goutor, *Guarding the Gates: The Canadian Labour Movement and Immigration, 1872–1934* (Vancouver: UBC Press, 2008).

278 *The Ledge*, April 19, 1905, p. 2; May 10, 1905, p. 2.

279 *Fernie Ledger*, September 7, 1907, p. 4.

280 *Fernie Free Press*, September 13, 1907, p. 4.

281 *Fernie Free Press*, February 8, 1907, p. 4; September 6, 1907, p. 1.

282 *District Ledger*, February 8, 1908, p. 8; February 15, 1908, p. 1.

283 *District Ledger*, June, July and August 1908.

284 *District Ledger*, April 18, 1908, p. 4; July 18, 1908, p. 1.

285 *District Ledger*, September 5, 1908, p. 8.

286 *District Ledger*, February 13 and 27, 1909, p. 8; May 15, 1909, p. 5.

287 *District Ledger*, May 29, 1909, p. 4; *Fernie Free Press*, March 1, 1901, p. 4; June 21, 1901, p. 4.

288 *Fernie Free Press*, May 28, 1909, p. 4.

289 *Fernie Free Press*, May 20, 1910, p. 1.

290 *Fernie Free Press*, March 17, 1905, p. 1; *The Ledge*, March 22, 1905, p. 2.

291 *Fernie Free Press*, February 18, 1910, p. 4; March 4, 1910, p. 4.

292 *Fernie Free Press*, March 11, 1910, p. 1; *District Ledger*, March 12, 1910, p. 1.

293 *Fernie Free Press*, August 5, 1910, p. 1; September 16, 1910, p. 6; August 11, 1911, p. 4.

294 *Henderson's British Columbia Gazetteer and Directory 1910*, Part One.

295 *District Ledger*, January 23, 1909, p. 5.

296 *Fernie Free Press*, December 12, 1903, p. 1. The advertisements (with an unfortunate and uncorrected typographical error) were discontinued after the fire of 1904.

297 *The Ledge*, May 10, 1905, p. 1; *Calgary Herald*, March 9, 1910, p. 7.

298 *District Ledger*, July 17, 1909, p. 8; *Fernie Free Press*, June 11, 1909, p. 5.

299   *Calgary Herald*, March 9, 1910, p. 7.

300   *Fernie Free Press*, April 7, 1905, p. 4.

301   *Fernie Free Press*, June 11, 1908, p. 1.

302   *Fernie Free Press*, March 15, 1912, p. 8.

303   George Pedlar is identified as editor between August 1908 and September 1912. Presumably *Free Press* owner John Wallace also contributed editorially, and there is no discernible difference in content before and after those dates. Wallace likely played an editorial role after he purchased the newspaper from Henderson in 1901, and Pedlar may have continued to assist after 1912.

304   The red-light district was located south of the Fernie city limits. *Fernie Free Press*, October 20, 1911, p. 4; August 22, 1913, p. 1; December 19, 1913, p. 1.

305   *Fernie Free Press*, November 20, 1914, p. 1.

306   After seven years of burial, the remains were cleaned and prepared for shipment to Harling Point in Victoria, in anticipation of a return to their home communities in China. See director Ling Chiu's *From Harling Point*, National Film Board of Canada, 2003; *Fernie Free Press*, August 16, 1918, p. 1.

307   FMA, City of Fernie Police Record; *Fernie Free Press*, February 22, 1918, p. 5; October 4, 1918, p. 5.

308   *Fernie Free Press*, March 5, 1920, p. 5; June 4, 1920, p. 5.

309   *Fernie Free Press*, May 28, 1924, p. 5.

310   *Wrigley's British Columbia Directory*, 1920 and 1921.

311   Wheta Chow was the first Chinese female to live in the Elk Valley. She joined her merchant husband at Natal in 1921. LAC, RG 76 D2a, General Registers of Chinese Immigration, 1885–1949. See https://central.bac-lac.gc.ca/.item/?id=e006069668&op=pdf&app=immigrantsfromchina.

312   *District Ledger*, February 20, 1909, p. 1; *Fernie Free Press*, November 14, 1913, p. 5; December 19, 1913, p. 1.

Pretty Good Stuff

313   *Fernie Free Press*, September 22, 1916, p. 1. Admittedly, at nearly 57 percent and 55 percent respectively, the ridings of Alberni and Newcastle were very close seconds. See *Port Alberni News*, October 4, 1916, p. 1, and *Ladysmith Chronicle*, September 16, 1916, p. 1.

314   For the controversies and final results, see Robert A. Campbell, *Demon Rum and Easy Money* (Ottawa: Carleton University Press, 1991), pp. 14–22.

315   Robert A. Campbell, *Demon Rum and Easy Money* (Ottawa: Carleton University Press, 1991), p. 31.

316   *Fernie Free Press*, October 22, 1920, p. 1.

317   *Fernie Free Press*, December 3, 1920, p. 1.

318   *Victoria Daily Times*, March 5, 1921, p. 3. Ironically, later in his political career, Scotch was known to be his drink of choice.

319   *Victoria Daily Times*, March 31, 1921, pp. 1, 3; *Victoria Daily Colonist*, April 1, 1921, pp. 1, 3.

320   RBCMA, British Columbia, Sessional Papers, *First Annual Report of the Liquor Control Board*, p. D23; Douglas L. Hamilton, *Sobering Dilemma: A History of Prohibition in British Columbia* (Vancouver: Ronsdale Press, 2004), p. 179; *Vancouver World*, June 15, 1921, p. 1.

321   For an appreciation of those restrictions and the culture of the beer parlour, see Robert A. Campbell, *Sit Down and Drink Your Beer* (Toronto: University of Toronto Press, 2001).

322   *Victoria Daily Times*, February 10, 1927, p. 5.

323   *Vancouver Province*, March 19, 1943, p. 15: *Vancouver Sun*, March 19, 1943, pp. 1, 14.

324   *Nelson Daily News*, April 12, 1943, p. 2.

325   *Fernie Free Press*, January 29, 1959, p. 1; February 26, 1959, p. 8.

326   For an assessment of that career, see Robert McDonald, "'Simply a Working Man': Tom Uphill of Fernie," in Wayne Norton and Tom Langford, eds., *A World Apart* (Kamloops, BC: Plateau Press, 2002), pp. 99–112.

327   The distinction of being the Empire's longest-serving politician in 1951 actually belonged to Harry Nixon. First elected to represent the provincial constituency of Brant in Ontario in 1919, Nixon also retired a year later than Uphill. For national and imperial political longevity, the MLA for Fernie remains in second place.

GLIMPSES OF DANGER

328   *District Ledger*, June 25, 1910, p. 5.

329   *Fourteenth Annual Report of the Provincial Board of Health*, British Columbia, Sessional Papers, 1912, pp. F16, 17.

330   Roger Stonebanks, *Fighting for Dignity: The Ginger Goodwin Story* (St John's: Canadian Committee on Labour History, 2004), pp. 25–29; *District Ledger*, October 1, 1910, p. 5. When Goodwin was killed in 1918, his medal was one of the few items in his possession. Alongside that of Arthur Boothman, the medal is now held at the Cumberland Museum.

331   *District Ledger*, February 7, 1914, p. 1.

332   Alf Budden was well known in socialist circles at the time. From North Battleford, Saskatchewan, he was identified as the SPC organizer for the province of Alberta in 1912. He spoke that year in Fernie, Michel and Hosmer, and was the unsuccessful SPC candidate for the Little Bow riding in the Alberta

provincial election of 1913. He began his 1914 speaking tour in Fernie with a lecture on the Paris Commune at the inaugural meeting in the new Socialist Hall on March 15, and often crossed paths with Goodwin over the next six weeks. Budden returned for another speaking tour of the region early in 1915, but soon thereafter seems to have disappeared from the historical record. See *District Ledger*, May 4, 1912, p. 2; June 22, 1912, p. 8; March 21, 1914, p. 4; January 16, 1915, p. 1.

333   *District Ledger*, February 28, 1914, p. 1.

334   *District Ledger*, February 28, 1914, p. 1.

335   *District Ledger*, March 7, 1914, p. 5. By 1914, the criticisms of 1910 concerning sanitation at Michel had been addressed by the Crow's Nest Pass Coal Company.

336   *District Ledger*, March 14, 1914, p. 5.

337   *District Ledger*, March 21, 1914, p. 5

338   *District Ledger*, March 14, 1914, p. 1.

339   *District Ledger*, April 18, p. 5.

340   *District Ledger*, April 25, 1914, p. 5. At Michel, Goodwin almost certainly met Herman Elmer, the like-minded local union secretary who would soon be charged with sedition and imprisoned.

341   *District Ledger*, April 25, 1914, p. 1; May 2, pp. 1, 5.

342   For an assessment of the internment crisis, see Wayne Norton, *Fernie at War: 1914–1919* (Halfmoon Bay, BC: Caitlin Press, 2017), pp. 50–72.

343   Susan Mayse, *Ginger: The Life and Death of Albert Goodwin* (Madeira Park, BC: Harbour Publishing, 1990), p. 89; *Fernie Free Press*, February 25, 1916, p. 1.

344   Goodwin to Premier Bowser, March 6, 1916, RBCMA, Premier, GR-0441, box 171, file 3; Roger Stonebanks, *Fighting for Dignity: The Ginger Goodwin Story* (St John's: Canadian Committee on Labour History, 2004), p. 64.

345   *Fernie Free Press*, March 11, 1899, p. 4.

Red Lights in Fernie

346   *Fernie Free Press*, May 6, 1899, p. 1

347   Henderson gave the case prominent coverage. *Fernie Free Press*, May 27, 1899, p. 1; June 3, 1899, p. 1; June 10, 1899, p. 5.

348   *Fernie Free Press*, August 4, 1899, pp. 1, 5.

349   *Fernie Free Press*, August 24, 1900, p. 5. These two houses probably came closest to approximating an establishment that might include a welcoming parlour, a well-stocked bar and perhaps a piano. For the story of restricted districts in the coal-mining communities of Lethbridge and Drumheller, see James Gray, *Red Lights on the Prairies* (Saskatoon, SK: Fifth House, 1971), pp. 175–205.

350   *Fernie Free Press*, May 27, 1899, p. 1.

351   RBCMA, County Court (Fort Steele) Civil Files, 1901–1905. GR 1603, box 1, file 1.

352   *Fernie Free Press*, October 11, 1901, p. 1. Mary Coffer (alias Mollie Rosencrantz) died intestate in Seattle in September 1901, leaving only the house in Fernie and its contents to be dealt with by an executor. RBCMA, Fort Steele County Court Probate/Estate Files. GR 1619.8, B09650(2).

353   *Fernie Free Press*, September 2, 1904, p. 4.

354   *The Ledge*, January 18, 1905, p. 1.

355   *Fernie Free Press*, May 13, 1904, p. 1; October 14, 1904, p. 1.

356   *Fernie Free Press*, December 2, 1910, p. 4.

357   *Fernie Free Press*, April 14, 1905, p. 1; June 23, 1905, p. 1; August 18, 1905, p. 1.

358   *Fernie Free Press*, August 10, 1906, p. 5; August 31, 1906, p. 1.

359   *Fernie Free Press*, May 29, 1908, p. 8.

360   *District Ledger*, May 23, 1908, p. 2; *Fernie Free Press*, July 17, 1908, p. 1; *Nanaimo Daily News*, August 4, 1908, p. 2.

361   *Calgary Herald*, August 5, 1908, p. 1. Lena Bell was also known as Melinda Leonard and Melissa Leonard. In the record of her unmarked burial site in the Fernie Heritage Cemetery and on her death registration (RBCMA, Division of Vital Statistics, GR 2951, volume 167, Death Registration 54679), she is identified as Melinda Leonard. The single reference to her as Melissa Leonard is in *Progressive Fernie*, p. 18. The death registration locates her house on Pellatt Avenue.

362   *Fernie Free Press*, October 30, 1908, p. 2.

363   *District Ledger*, October 17, 1908, p. 6.

364   *District Ledger*, November 14, 1908, p. 4; *The Prospector*, December 12, 1908, p. 6.

365   *District Ledger*, December 5, 1908, p. 2.

366   *District Ledger*, January 9, 1909, p. 4; Mayor Sherwood Herchmer to Attorney General William Bowser, November 26, 1910, RBCMA, Attorney General, box 18, file 4, folio 6889.

367   *District Ledger*, November 21, 1908, p. 1; November 28, 1908, p. 1; January 9, 1909, p. 6; January 16, 1909, p. 1.

368   FMA, City of Fernie Police Book, 1909–1912. An administrative charge of $1 was always added to each fine imposed in police court.

369   Mayor Sherwood Herchmer to Attorney General William Bowser, November 26, 1910, RBCMA, British Columbia, Attorney General, box 18, file 4, folio 6889.

370   *District Ledger*, November 12, 1910, p. 1; *Fernie Free Press*, November 11, 1910, p. 4; November 18, 1910, p. 6; December 2, 1910, p. 4.

371   *Victoria Daily Times*, September 27, 1911, p. 1.

372   *Fernie Free Press*, June 20, 1913, p. 1.

373   FMA, City of Fernie Police Record, 1912–1923.

374   Also in 1916, Presbyterians and Methodists in Fernie—agreeing on matters social and theological—voted almost unanimously to merge their congregations, but were prevented from doing so by the Methodist parent body. Two years later, a second attempt proved successful. See Wayne Norton, *Fernie at War: 1914–1919* (Halfmoon Bay, BC: Caitlin Press, 2017), pp. 102–103, 145.

375   Report of Constable Charles Kerr, February 1917, RBCMA, Provincial Police Force, GR-0445, box 37, file 4; *Fernie Free Press*, February 16, 1917, p. 1.

376   *Fernie Free Press*, March 16, 1917, p. 1; March 23, 1917, p. 1.

377   *Fernie Free Press*, March 23, 1917, p. 5.

378   *Fernie Free Press*, April 6, 1917, p. 1; FMA, City of Fernie Police Record, 1912–1923.

379   *Fernie Free Press*, August 17, 1917, pp. 1, 5.

380   Report of Chief Constable George Welsby, December 1917, RBCMA, Provincial Police Force, GR-0445, box 37, file 12; *Fernie Free Press*, January 4, 1918, p. 5.

381   *Fernie Free Press*, June 27, 1919, p. 1.

ABOUT THE AUTHOR

Wayne Norton was born in Calgary, raised as an Air Force brat in Canada and Scotland, and now lives in Victoria, BC. Wayne's teaching career in British Columbia and England involved classes ranging from kindergarten to Grade 12 in subjects such as music, special education and history. More recently, he worked as a research consultant for the Indian Residential School Resolution Process. With degrees in history from Simon Fraser University and the University of British Columbia, Wayne enjoys exploring neglected topics. In his many published books and articles Wayne has delved into Canadian music from the Great War, women's ice hockey, public health, and the local histories of Kamloops and Fernie. His most recent book, *Fernie at War: 1914-1919*, won the Community History Award from the BC Historical Federation. Wayne is a member of historical associations in Victoria and Fernie. He notes that his three young grandchildren continue to delight—even as they remind him how quickly time passes.